I'LL TAKE THIS WORD AND MAKE IT MINE

I'll Take This Word and Make It Mine

2018-2019
California
Poets in the Schools
Statewide Anthology

California Poets in the Schools
Santa Rosa

First Edition.
ISBN 978-0-939927-29-6
Library of Congress Control Number: 2019949132

The book's title, *I'll Take This Word and Make it Mine* is a line from the poem, "Call Me Chicano" by Angelina Leanos.

Cover Artist: Isabelle Montagne, Grade 3, Santa Cruz County, CA

Chapter headings are lines from these poems: *I am Alive,* from "I am a Piece of a Cloud" by Aiden Reinhard; *A Hundred Hairs of a Fox,* from "A Violin" by Orion Gainsforth; *Infinity is the Name of My Soul,* from "Infinity" by Donovan Topete Alvarado; *The Forest is Waiting for Me,* from "The Forest Mother" by Kika Dunayovich; *And if There Were No Rainbows,* from "Rain is Falling" by Maya Trockel; *If Poetry Was a Color,* from "If Poetry" by Seagrin Lawless; *A Blessing to the Paper,* from "Mr. Pen" by Asha Nayak; *My Compass Doesn't Do What a Compass Does,* from "My Weird Compass" by Sylvia Harsh; *A Way of Life that Only the Stars Understand,* from "Morning Glory" by Adele Robbins.

California Poets in the Schools
P.O. Box 1328, Santa Rosa, CA 95402
415-221-4201
info@cpits.org
https://www.californiapoets.org
Meg Hamill, Executive Director
Magdalena Montagne, Editor
Brennan DeFrisco, Assistant Editor
Kate Hitt, Editing & Design

(Fonts: Minion Text with Ashley Script Titling)

California Poets in the Schools is generously supported by
The California Arts Council

Dedication

California Poets in the Schools, now in its fifty-fifth year, owes a debt of gratitude to our talented and devoted Poet-Teachers, as they carry on teaching with passion and commitment, giving so many students voice through poetry. We dedicate this anthology to them, and especially to the poets we have lost over the years.

Note from the Editor

When writing a poem, "put in lots of stuff,"Academy of American Poets Chancellor Ellen Bass once said. As you read through this 2019 anthology of student poems, you will be amazed (as I was) at the sheer number of objects—so many things to write about after all!

Certainly the work of a poet starts here: observing the physical world and our relationship to objects/events/experiences. I can recall vividly still, after all these years, my eleven-year-old self writing my first poem—an unlikely ode to the moon on a humid New Jersey summer's evening. This sense of awakening is here, along with wonder…and exuberance.…

Throughout the anthology, many students take on tough questions and this makes me feel particularly grateful for the sanctity of poetry. These students ask: Who am I? What is my place? Do I belong? Does it make a difference? For all "students of life" these questions remain with us, perhaps ultimately unanswerable. Yet, poetry affords us the vehicle to ask and to lead us to where healing and wholeness begin.

The poet's task: Examine, reflect, proclaim: I AM.

As you enter this world of imagination, exploration, fantasy and dreams, consider how the world grows larger because of these poems. How we are asked to expand, and in so doing form a great circle that encompasses both the light and darkness, from joy to sorrow and everything in between.

May the poet within us all rise up to greet these younger poets and celebrate their outstanding courage and fortitude and success with each of those poems.

Thank you for reading!

Magdalena Montagne, October, 2019

Foreword

by John Fox

Octavio Paz said a long while ago, "Poetry is not a very popular art form but it is an essential part of life."

That late great poet of Mexico speaks to us, today. He might even say, given the profoundly precarious cultural travail and national trauma of enduring such inhumane federal policies at our southern border, that poetry is more than essential.

If we are to make it to some other side, without losing our soul, poetry is *necessary* to that survival, to making it through. By the "other side," I mean that place which reclaims and treasures language, the imagination and truth-telling.

We need to see and declare that place. We need to escape our timidity about poetry and hungrily gather poems into mind, body and soul.

A testimonial usually has choice adjectives to stir a reader to excitement, even enthusiasm. The thought is—if I can strike the right adjective, as if it were a match, a flint—I can spark an ember in your heart that will inspire you to buy this book and take it home.

Even though I believe this double-anthology (two years of CalPoets' poems!) *I'll Take This Word and Make It Mine* is indeed *spectacular*—I am going to lean into the necessity of it.

> The easiest thing is to lose your truth,
> but if you do, what will become of you?
>
> —*Xoana Zamudio-Truncos, 4th grade*

Yes, yes!… what will become of us if we lose our truth? Xoana, nine years old, has every right to ask. We would do well to sit down and listen. You and I could listen to this child, this wise one. We could listen to this one:

The golden blossom
has secrets to tell you:
how to glow deep
in the world.

—Shengxi Huang, 3rd grade

This book of poems will help you glow deep in your world. And
beyond that glowing, I advise you to feel your feet on the ground
and receive this storm of feeling:

What about all the people working in the fields,
Picking fruit for you dammit?
What about people like us who want to succeed,
Who would if you just gave us a chance?
What about people like me?
I am not a number.
I have a name.

—Angelina Leanos, 12th grade

These poems are wise, lovely and fierce. They are playful-silly, just
right sweet and mind-blowing. They enter the heart as if to
remind us, at last, that *all of life* itself is made for that very
place—the heart. I especially like this one:

If I could go to a Lost and Found, and find someone,
I would find my great grandma, and watch the World Series
with her.

—Carter Low, 6th grade

This book could very well be your lost and found. I trust you will
find a poem in these pages that has gone missing and now, returns
to you. Maybe these next lines will feel like ones you wish could be
yours:

My heart is made of kittens that are meowing
and waves crashing on the beach.

—Emily Gore, 1st grade

Before I close, I want to give a BIG SHOUT OUT to the Poet-Teachers who show up with such love and dedication to invite, inspire and receive these poems. They are, each of them, so remarkable and fine. Twenty-eight years ago I had the good fortune to come into contact with California Poets in the Schools. I taught for many years, mostly in the South Bay. My mentor was the revered Lu Melander.

That yellow pencil logo that reminds me of the sun helped to light my way for a life of poetry and healing. It was shining then as now.

Kindness,

John Fox
Founder, The Institute for Poetic Medicine
Author of *Finding What You Didn't Lose: Expressing Your Truth and Creativity Through Poem-Making.*

P. S. I woke up with this thought—my foreword isn't quite done. All of these poems were, at least initially, written with others. They were written—each so unique—within the community of the classroom. I imagine these poems were heard together. These children and teens spoke up—and listened to one another. Imagine that.

Table of Contents

Note From the Editor, Magdalena Montagne

Foreword by John Fox

I Am Alive

Loved Ones, Angel Rodriguez,   1
The Path to Remember, Gloria Lopez,   2
My Heart's Book of Records, Inara Miller,   3
I Am, Nomiah Britton,   4
I Am the Cat, Ready to Pounce, Alex Gosselin,   5
I Am the String That Shoots the Arrow, Zayar Dorku, 6
I Am a Piece of a Cloud, Aiden Reinhard,   7
I Am Autistic, Wyatt Mesker,   8
The Abundant World, Leandro German,   9
I Am a Wolf Inside, Jackson Tipton,   10
I Am the Wolf, Finn Felicich,   11
I Am Earth, Paloma Cordrey,   12
Egyptian Hieroglyphic, Jack Laughlin,   13
I, Chloe Haines Sobolewski,   14
Me, Bryleigh Redner,   15
90 Percent, Jose P.,   17
Sweat, Tears, and Blood, Kody I.,   18
Spirit of the Night, Elizabeth Alvarado,   19
Lea, Finley Robinson,   20
The Princess of Spring, Genesis Canales,   21
I Love My Heart!, Emily Gore,   22
Passover, Zoe Rocco-Zilber,   23
We Are China, Joey Lau,   24
Culture, Luan Shrivner,   25
The Fields of Vietnam, Khloe Phan,   26
I Come From An Island Adrift in the Pacific,
                              Ashley Glancy,   27
Call Me Chicano, Angelina Leanos,   30
I Am From…, Lilly Long,   32
2 Languages, Raul Soto,   33
Directions to My Home, My Heart, Breyana Wright, 34
My Hands Are Helpful, Jordan Castañeda,   35
Self Portrait, Ben Smith,   36
Perspective, Eli Charles Griffen,   37

A Hundred Hairs of A Fox   39

I Wonder What the Animals Would Say, Eliya Yavi, 40
It's Raining Rats and Cats, Rowan Carr,   42
Golden Dog, Ashlynn Orsi,   43
Crab, Arman Entezari,   44
The Great Harris' Hawk, Willis Cardot,   45
A Goodbye Day for the Mosquito Eater,
                              Katelyn Burbec, 46
Dragons, Leif Swenson,   47
Animals in the Jungle, Ronan Corbit,   48
Bald Eagle Rap, Jamal Hewitt,   49
Tiger's Breath & Dragons, Rafferty Kan,   51

Crow, Charlee Cate Cardot,   53
Spring Wolf, Kylie Luna,   54
Ocelot, Jude Park,   55
Gorillas, Yamila Esper,   56
The Snowdrift Penguin, Ali Post,   57
El Oso, Adán Baquiax,   58
The Bandit, Isabella Schlitt,   59
Bird, Rosie Murray,   62
Smoke of the Wind, Ava Baldwin Ferguson,   63
The Fox, Judith Pina,   64
Dear Wolf, Amirah McGee,   65
The Life of a Cat, Jasmine Morton,   66
Happiness, Amy Arenal,   67
Phoenix, Arisbet Camacho,   68
Pegasus, Joshua Gomez,   69
I See You, Eric Domingue,   70
Winter, Genevive Briceno,   71

Infinity is the Name of My Soul   73

Infinity, Donovan Topete Alvarado,   74
You Are Mine, Savina Hamm,   75
Let It Live, Maya Huiza,   77
When I Listen, Josie Morris,   79
Most Beautiful, Blooma Goldberg,   80
La Felicidad, Brayan Camay,   81
Portrait of Joy, Ryan Martin,   82
Gracefulness, Alice Johnson,   83
Wonder, Xoana Zamudio-Truncos,   84
Courage, Adam Gelfand,   85
I Believe in the Wind, Jaida Steinebaugh,   86
Free, Margaret Eglin,   87
Balloons, Anjali Bose,   88
Me Haces Volar, Daryhan Cardozo,   89
More To The Heart, Isaac Piñon,   90
In the Heart of Myself, Shengxi Huang,   91
Back In Balance, Tiger Han,   93
Goddesses Have To Eat Too, Margaret Farley,   94
Angels in the Sky, Pria Kussat,   95
The Angel with a Mustache, Natalia Stafford,   97
The Voice, Cameron Huffman,   98
My Secret Place, Jack Conway,   99
On the Other Side of Tomorrow,
                              Aidan Hursh, 100
Change, Rosie McWhorter,   101
Fire in the Savannah, Alyssa Hughes,   102
Dying Heart, Noah Swanson,   103
Lazy Sunday, Leo Beach,   104
Calm, Seagrin Lawless,   105
To Be the Change, Pearl McKay,   106
Changes, Hazel Dale,   107
Mad Hatter, Wyatt Kennedy,   108
Tomorrow, Caitlin O'Donnell,   109
I Don't Know, Phaedra Steadman,   110

Table of Contents, Continued

My World, Nadya Brodetsky, 111
Friends, Eleanore Schiro, 112
Friendship, Sarah Morse, 113
My Family, Lewanna Le, 114
Ode to My Sister, Gwen Chenoweth, 115
My Sister Is Waiting For Me, Kayden Hawks, 116
My Brother Antonio, Kamila Flores, 117
My Dad, Magid Reboug, 118
Nanny and Papa, Joscelyn Beebe, 119
Great Grandma Marie, Carter Low, 120
Songbird, Jaxi Cohen, 121
Back Through My Life, Mason Spessard, 122
Remember When, Isaiah Case, 125

The Forest is Waiting For Me 127

The Forest Mother, Kika Dunayevic, 128
A Cool Summer Day, Hali Wight, 129
Blue White Feather, Colby Thomson, 130
The Taste of Plants, Grace Monaghan, 132
The Cherry Blossom, Yuki Wen, 133
On The Hill Over Yonder, Amelia Noble, 135
Acorn, Ahtyirahm Allen, 136
Broken Aspen, Isabella Schlitt, 137
Morning Glory, Adele Robbins, 138
Snoglehopher, Luke Fosse, 139
Anti-Ode to Sand, Alia Prentiss, 140
Field of Whispers Heard, Maya Looney, 141
Point Reyes, California, Koa Wessner, 142
If Point Reyes Was A Person, Zoë Rocco-Zilber, 143
Sunrise, Kongtae Kaewasalam, 144
The Sun Above Me, Charlotte Perry, 145
Cotton from the Clouds, Paloma Rudnicki, 146
Above the Clouds, Kaidance W., 147
Moon Musings, Daniela Lopez Arreguin, 148
Box, Riley Houston, 150
How Stars Exist in a Crazy Way
                    Daniel Bustamante, 152
Stars, Lea Anderson, 153
What the Night Hears, Madison Meredith, 154
Nature's Music, Cole Jayme, 155
Silvery Golden Sounds, Allie Andresen, 156
The Sky, Austin Presley, 157
Give Me A Planet Like Pluto, Ryan Wu, 158
The Living Planet, Summer Hurst, 159
How to Be Fire, Truett Sheehy, 160
Fire, Catherine Petty, 161
Water, Cadence Lu, 162
The Spirit of Water, Stela Clark, 163
It's Raining Very Hard, Emily Silva, 164

Rain is Falling, Amaya Trockel, 165
Rain, Clodagh McIntyre, 166

And If There Were No Rainbows 167

My Heart, Marleena Limbrick, 168
Her Mind, Delilah Tarr, 169
Shy, Aubrey Pine, 170
Shyness, Max Pasquale, 171
Envy, Ariel Reyes, 172
Sad Life, Nya Flynn, 173
Fear is Like a Window, Ella Rose von Junsch, 174
Fear Is a Teenage Boy, Vinnie Hamann, 175
Loneliness, Haven Armistead, 176
Loneliness Is Like a World With No People,
                    Bristahl Adams, 177
Pain, Violet Castillo-Osman, 178
When I Am..., Alexie Gutierrez, 179
Dark Walks Alone, Joey Jimenez, 180
That Was Then, Anonymous, 181
Enough, Skye Torres, 182
Blood Stone, Nora Ross, 183
Death's Door, Everett Gallagher, 184
Remember, Nanami Fuller, 185
Worries, Worries All Comin' Up, Emily Walsh, 186
Lunacy, Genesis Perez, 188
La Verguenza, Brandon Tamayo, 189
Spirit, Philippa McKevitt, 190
Have You Ever Left Someone? Alaa Al-Badani, 191
Imagina, Cesar Jarquin Flores, 192
Placement, Caitlin O'Donnell, 193
Lost Time, Jadyn Fenyves-Ward, 194
Drama, Calypso Olstad, 195
Culture, Kai Gao, 196
Where You From?, Gio L., 197
Pocho, Carlos G., 198
Pony Tail, Kody I., 199
No Es La Luna, Luis A., 200
me, Diego V., 201
Safe Place, Cody M., 202
On Meditation, Aleah F., 203
Locked Up, Giovanni L., 204
I Would Fly Away, Bryan G., 205
Facil/Easy, Bryan S, 206
Unique, Ella Hobson, 207
Our Country, Natalie Banton, 209
The Cage We Made, Amon B. Chavez, 210
the long ride, Emma Crowe, 211
The Questions, DeAngelo Martinez, 213
LA Poem, Philippa McKevitt, 214
The Marigold Sun, Jaxi Cohen, 216

Table of Contents, Continued

If Poetry Was a Color   219

Poem Soda, Carlos Duffield,	220
Only a Poem, Cruz , Gattnar,	221
Mr. Pen, Asha Nayak,	222
The Words of History, Greta LaFemina,	223
Long and Short, Victoria Lewis,	224
Bad Poem, Finn Talley,	225
Not My Strong Suit, Jaxon Craig,	226
Tucked Away, Clara Watson,	227
My Poem, Stephanie Uraga,	228
The Book Was…, Andrea Diaz,	229
Book, Baylee Carpenter,	230
Books, Elliot Abrahams,	231
If Poetry, Seagrin Lawles,	232
Feeling Colors, Avery Simington,	233
Blue's Feelings, Livia Corea,	234
Baby Blue, Davey Hipes,	235
Sky and Sea, Fritz Moss,	236
Blue, Cadence Lu,	237
Black, Colton Schaefer,	238
Red in Music, Edward Lopez,	239
Gold, Elana Rowan,	240
Ode to Brown, Kacy Truc-Vy Kramer,	241
Blue's Lament, Akasha Bowen,	242
Gypsy Caravan Turquoise, Gemma Geldert,	243

A Blessing to the Paper: Ekphrastic Poems   245

The Jimson Weed, Kiran Thole,	246
Mexico, Zana Schreie,	247
The Grand Canyon, Parker Richardson,	248
A Couple Dining Midair, Tucker Wojdowski,	249
The Tree, Ben Stone,	250
Autumn Fire Tree, Wyatt Mesker,	251
Spotted Dog, Kylie Peterson,	252
Brussels Sprouts, Cade Moharram,	253
Chagall, Britta Thornal,	254
Suzanne Collins, Jake Wedemeyer,	255
The Great Wave Haiku, Josue Muñoz,	256
The Persistence of Memory, Myrna Escamilla,	257
Cape Cod Morning, Nico Ingargiola,	258
On the Other Side of the Painting, Jocelyn Coultré	259
Lightning Bolt, Arianna Ramos,	260

My Compass Doesn't Do What a Compass Does 261

My Weird Compass, Sylvia Harsh,	262
The Museum of Broken Things, Sarah Kemper,	263
Green Shirt, Massimo Bonilla-Zakosek,	264

To My Braces, Hazel Heckes,	265
Sounds Like…, Avery Simington,	266
The Flattest Thing, Lawler Jackson,	267
The Tea Book, Delia Moss,	268
Ode to the Garbage Can, Addison Everage,	269
Quotidian Cube, Georgia Schreiner,	270
A Violin, Orion Gainsforth,	272
The Life of Music, Madison Reagan Leedy,	273
To Make an Orchestra, Uma Anandakuttan,	274
Origin of Tennis, Delilah Rain Sheehan,	275
Opposites, Clayton Hunter,	276

A Way of Life That Only the Stars Understand:
Poet-Teacher Poems   277

Backyard Vista of the Bird Fiesta, Terri Glass,	278
Cross-Pollination, Brian Kirven,	279
Rayo Verde, Brian Kirven,	280
Beach Run, Alice Pero,	281
Grand Canyon, Megan Young,	282
Blessing for the Laguna de Santa Rosa Trail,	
Jackie Huss Hallerberg	284
Daughter, Seretta Martin,	286
In My Daughter's House,	
Phyllis Meshulam	287
Ninguno Menos Rosa/None Less a Rose,	
Jabez Churchill	288
Playing With Dolls, Claire Blotter,	290
Bounty, Beth Beurkens,	291
A Visit with Grandma, Sandra Anfang,	293
I Live Extreme, Jessica M. Wilson,	294
Evangelio, Jabez W. Churchill,	295
Mice, Amanda Chiado,	297
The Happy Poem, Amanda Chiado,	298
Writer's Workshop Haiku, Lisa Shulman,	299
On Reading Poetry in Tight Spaces,	
Lisa Shulman,	301
Out Loud, Brennan DeFrisco,	302
how poems spring to life,	
Lalli Dana Drobny,	303
Did the Flower Know, Julie Hochfeld,	305
Vacant Eyes Reflect, Pamela Singer,	306
A Yoga Summer, Linden Berry,	307
I Have Thought of You, Young Poets,	
Lois Klein,	308
Our Mission	
Who We Are	
Board of Directors, Advisory Council, Staff	
Owl (Concrete Poem) Avery Knight Blankfort,	317

I AM ALIVE

Loved Ones

Remember the rhino that lost its horns.
   Remember how painful that was for him.
Remember the days you have had.
   Remember how they made you happy.
Remember your family. Remember the food they make for you.
   Think of how grateful you should be that you have a home.
   Think of how sad the homeless are and how you can help.
Remember the disaster you survived and how grateful you are
   to still be alive.
Remember the people who are sad about the things they lost.
Then, remember how glad you are to still have your loved ones.

ANGEL RODRIGUEZ, 5TH GRADE
BROOKS ELEMENTARY SCHOOL, SONOMA COUNTY
PATTI DEARTH, CLASSROOM TEACHER
JACKIE HUSS HALLERBERG, POET-TEACHER

The Path to Remember

Remember the time, the first time you opened your eyes, the
time you were born.
Remember the origin of your skin, what's in your blood.
Remember the Mexican dishes your mother struggled to cook.
Remember your education and how much value it actually has.
Remember your life and how many times you have been
happy, upset, mad, brave
and just fine.
Your life is a gift and there are many paths to choose from.
I choose the path to remember the past in the present.

GLORIA LOPEZ, 5TH GRADE
BROOKS ELEMENTARY SCHOOL
PATTI DEARTH, CLASSROOM TEACHER
JACKIE HUSS HALLERBERG, POET-TEACHER

My Heart's Book of Records

The quietest thing is the wolves howling in the night.
The sweetest thing is my scars finally healing.
The noisiest thing is the thunder and lightning when Zeus is angry.
The tallest thing is the pile of books on my desk.
The wisest thing is Athena's owls hooting as they dive.
The brightest thing is my best friend's smile when he sees me.
The truest thing is the bond of friendship.
The slowest thing is my tortoise walking through deep sand.
The bravest person is my friend when someone hurts one of us.
The saddest thing is my best friend when he stares into my soul
    and I know that I may never see him again.

INARA MILLER, 4TH GRADE
BROOKS ELEMENTARY SCHOOL, SONOMA COUNTY
SCOTT ANDERTON, CLASSROOM TEACHER
JACKIE HUSS HALLERBERG, POET-TEACHER

I Am

I am
Exactly what I want to be in this moment,
I am
The smile you see looking back at you.
I am not
Those names you whisper under your breath.
You may think I am,
but I am not.
I am not
the reminder of what has happened.
I am not
the past.
I am
a different person, from who I was 5 minutes
ago.
I am not perfect.
I am the future.
See ME.

NOMIAH BRITTON
GRADE 10, WILLITS HIGH SCHOOL, MENDOCINO COUNTY
AMY NORD, CLASSROOM TEACHER
PJ FLOWERS, POET-TEACHER

I Am The Cat, Ready to Pounce

I am the cat, ready to pounce.
I am a volcano, ready to erupt with joy.
I am a tree, full of new spring leaves.
I am the wind, making happiness for the world.
I am our moon, shining down on us.
I am a great clear lagoon, singing with beauty.
I am our sun, lightening us past darkness.
I am one of billions of stars
    trying to find its way.
I am our life, finding our destiny.
I am a soldier doing what we think is right.
I am a planet, swirling around life,
    never ending our friendship.
I am the rainforest making home to the wild.
I am the fruit trees, ready to share the great
    tastes of the world.
I am a snake, searching for prey.
I am a hurricane, great winds that bring peace.
I am the four seasons, weather full of pride.
I am the great and beautiful life of everything.
I am all of it.

ALEX GOSSELIN, 3RD GRADE
PRESTWOOD ELEMENTARY, SONOMA COUNTY
ELLIE KATZEL, CLASSROOM TEACHER
SANDRA ANFANG, POET-TEACHER

I Am The String That Shoots the Arrow

I am the string that shoots the arrow.
I am the sea that crashes on the cliff.
I am what you think I am not.
I am the gorilla who defended his family.
I am the one who painted his horse.
I am the howl that came out of the jackal.
I am the one who led his people to victory.
I am the rock that tumbled down the tepetl (mountain).
I am the dorku (turkey in Ghanian) who gobbled.
I am the person who united man, woman, and small people.
I am the one who survived the ta moko (Maori tattooing).
I am the pond that formed in the rocky kemet (Egyptian for desert).
I can be anything that I say, anything I don't say.
When I go, people will remember me with this.

ZAYAR DORKU, 3RD GRADE
PRESTWOOD ELEMENTARY, SONOMA COUNTY
CARLY COSTELLO, CLASSROOM TEACHER
SANDRA ANFANG, POET-TEACHER

I Am a Piece of a Cloud

I am a piece of a cloud
I am the road screaming out loud
I am the sun shining so bright
I am the wind calling it a night
I am a gun shooting the sign
I am the dust in the night
I am rain saying my pain
I am the sky
You see, I am alive, I am alive

Aiden Reinhard, 3rd grade
Delphi Academy, Los Angeles County
Ann Swapp, Classroom Teacher
Alice Pero, Poet-Teacher

I Am Autistic

I am Autistic
I wonder why
I see things differently
I want people to like me
I am Autistic

I worry that people will judge me
I cry about that
I am Autistic

I understand that I'm different
I say nobody's perfect
I dream that others believe that too
I try to believe it myself
I am Autistic

WYATT MESKER, 4TH GRADE
POINSETTIA ELEMENTARY, VENTURA COUNTY
DIANE SATHER AND JULIE SOSKE, CLASSROOM TEACHERS
JENNIFER KELLEY, POET-TEACHER

The Abundant World

I am a hyena of light that hunts down what keeps you up at night
I am a lotus flower that hides its fragrance –
    I will show myself only if you have patience
I am the cool drizzle on a hot sunny day
I am a star next to the moonlight to reflect your beauty
I am the creek gone silent so I can hear you
I am your guardian angel

LEANDRO GERMAN, 6TH GRADE
ROSELAND ELEMENTARY SCHOOL, SONOMA COUNTY
MS. SLONGA, CLASSROOM TEACHER
JACKIE HUSS HALLERBERG, POET-TEACHER

I Am a Wolf Inside

I am a wolf inside
I wonder what spiritual prayers I will catch
I hear the voices of the wind all around me
I see the prey running away as I chase it
I want to be alpha of the pack
I am a wolf inside

I pretend to be the best wolf
I feel the vibrations of my wolf ancestors
I touch the bright white cold snow
I worry if I will ever be hunted by hunters
I cry for victory
I am a wolf inside

I understand that I will leave this world
I say that I am alpha
I dream of reaching my hunting goals
I try to learn the way of the wolf
I hope for my heart to be in the right place
I am a wolf inside

JACKSON TIPTON, 4TH GRADE
POINSETTIA ELEMENTARY, VENTURA COUNTY
DIANE SATHER AND JULIE SOSKE, CLASSROOM TEACHERS
JENNIFER KELLEY, POET-TEACHER

I Am the Wolf

I am the wolf
with fur like lightning.

I am the wolf
with a howl like the wind.

I am the wolf
with a stomp like an earthquake.

I am the wolf
as fast as a jet.

Finn Felicich, 5th grade
Mendocino K-8 Elementary, Mendocino County
Beth Renslow, Classroom Teacher
Hunter Gagnon, Poet-Teacher

I Am... Earth

I am the green
of the trees.
I am the sturdiness
of the grounds.
I am the chocolate
in the cocoa.
I am the love
in being together.
I am the heart
in the sweet puppy.
I am the surprise
in the experiment.
I am the wave
in the sea.
I am the flame
coming from the ashes.
I am the bud
before the flower.
I am the water droplets
in the air,
for nature is me.

PALOMA CORDREY, 4TH GRADE
WEST MARIN SCHOOL, MARIN COUNTY
ANNE HALLEY-HARPER, CLASSROOM TEACHER
BRIAN KIRVEN, POET-TEACHER

(Egyptian hieroglyphic)

I am the sea churning,
enveloping lost travelers
in my abysmal depths.
I am a road meandering,
uncertain of my destination.
I am a fence, an assuring
border, imprisoning those
seeking false safety within
my refuge.

JACK LAUGHLIN, 12TH GRADE
MADRONE HIGH SCHOOL, MARIN COUNTY
ALEXIS MORGAN, CLASSROOM TEACHER
LEA ASCHKENAS, POET-TEACHER

I

I'm like an antique violin.
My music is beautiful
But I'm fragile

I'm like a game of chess
You just can't seem to win me

I'm like a poster on the wall
You can always find me

I'm like the only leaf
on the ground in one area
I'm different from others

I'm like the season of winter
in Humboldt County
I can't quite decide
what I want to do

I'm like my cat
I'll leave
then come back
shortly after

I'm like the week
I have good days
and bad ones

I'm like a pair of glasses
The ones who need me
don't want me

Chloe Haines Sobolewski, 5th grade
Pacific Union School, Humboldt Co.
Cheryl Paul, Classroom Teacher
Daryl Ngee Chinn, Poet-Teacher

14

Me

I am like a path
leading and following

I am like a word
always being misspelled

I am like an ice skate
making it possible
to travel forward and back
and making it fun

I am like a dolphin
leaping and dancing before dawn

I am like a word
some boring and some interesting

I am like a three-toed sloth
Small

I am like a pencil working
and working for something I want

I am like an eraser
always wanting
for things to be perfect

I am like a pencil grip
held onto for help

I am like watercolors

Light and dark
and middle shades
drifting across my paper

I am like a hula hoop
going around
until it stops

I am like a baton twirler
Waiting and practicing
'til things go right
Because I work hard
and I like competitions

Because I love what I do
and so should you

I am like a butterfly
leaping across the sky
flying
and fun to watch

I am like gum
stuck in someone's hair
Sticky sticky stuck

I am like a butterfly
Small, nice
What are you like?

BRYLEIGH REDNER, 5TH GRADE
PACIFIC UNION SCHOOL, HUMBOLDT CO.
CHERYL PAUL, CLASSROOM TEACHER
DARYL NGEE CHINN, POET-TEACHER

90 Percent

90%
guerrero
90%
sobreviviente.
El fuego que llevas adentro
viene del fondo,
muy debajo de la tierra.
Explota de la muerte
y demustra tu poder.

90%
warrior
90%
survivor.
The fire you carry inside
comes from deep,
deep underground,
erupts from death,
will show your strength.

JOSE P., 11TH GRADE
WEST HILLS SCHOOL, MENDOCINO COUNTY
DIANA BLUNDELL, CLASSROOM TEACHER
JABEZ W. CHURCHILL, POET-TEACHER

Sweat, Tears, and Blood

Warriors sweat in lodges
for bad spirits to come out.
Shed tears of joy and passing,
not in pain.
They don't feel pain.
Warriors' blood
putting in work
for new generations.

KODY I., 12TH GRADE
WEST HILLS SCHOOL, MENDOCINO COUNTY
DIANA BLUNDELL, CLASSROOM TEACHER
JABEZ W. CHURCHILL, POET-TEACHER

Spirit of the Night

I'm the sound of the wind
that passes through you
I pass through the colorful
field of flowers
I breeze in your hair
I run with you
I am the soul of the wind

I am the light of lightning
flashing through your life
I am the thunder flashing out
over the dark empty land
I flash through your eyes

I am the Spirit of the Night
My eyes are made of sleepy moonlight
Stars roll down my cheeks
My quiet voice spills from my mouth
I love to give you my night dreams
I speak of the peaceful hooting owl

ELIZABETH ALVARADO, 5TH GRADE
VENETIA VALLEY SCHOOL, MARIN COUNTY
ELI PARIS, CLASSROOM TEACHER
PRARTHO SERENO, POET-TEACHER

Lea

I am Lea, the goddess of the sea.
My eyes are made of shiny silver fish.
I see coral reefs and kids running in my waves.
I look at my waves as they play with the wind.
I cry cold salty water.
My best friend is Ariana, the goddess of love.
My robe is made of mermaid tears and songs.
My home is in the Dead Sea
in a house of the deepest blue in the sea.
My pet is a dolphin with gold stripes on her back.
She has dark black eyes,
like deep holes that never stop.

FINLEY ROBINSON, 3RD GRADE
PARK SCHOOL, MARIN COUNTY
JOE MARTINI, CLASSROOM TEACHER
PRARTHO SERENO, POET-TEACHER

The Princess of Spring

I am the Princess of Spring
You will meet me at the Rain Tree,
in the rain storms I sing

You can see a Queen of Love
No one can love me, flowers are on me

I make the leaves on the trees and plants
Frogs play on my blue leaves

In the summer I sleep
No one can wake me up

Spring is my mother—
No one loves Spring like me
I am the Princess of Spring

GENESIS CANALES, 3RD GRADE
VENETIA VALLEY SCHOOL, MARIN COUNTY
ALEXANDRIA WINSTON, CLASSROOM TEACHER
PRARTHO SERENO, POET-TEACHER

I Love My Heart!

My heart is made of kittens that are meowing
and waves crashing against the beach.
It is filled with bright sunlight warming me.
You can hear a wolf howling at the moonlight
and the pencil sketching across the paper
and the wind howling at me.
There are deer running in the wetlands.
There are raccoons peering at me with their yellow eyes.

EMILY GORE, 1ST GRADE
STRAWBERRY POINT SCHOOL, MARIN COUNTY
KIMBERLY RUSSEL, CLASSROOM TEACHER
PRARTHO SERENO, POET-TEACHER

Passover

I am
a story
I am
a mystery in
a jar
I am an 11 o'clock Seder
I am the salty tears
of slaves waiting, waiting
more waiting
I am the souls of stories
I am family around a table
I am blood on doorways
I am the death of the
first born son
I am the voice
of Gods and Angels
Dying people
Living slaves
Happiness
Regrets
Thankfulness
The Promised Land
Death
I am Passover

ZOE ROCCO-ZILBER, 5TH GRADE
WEST MARIN SCHOOL, MARIN COUNTY
ESTHER UNDERWOOD, CLASSROOM TEACHER
BRIAN KIRVEN, POET-TEACHER

We Are China

I came from the breath of life.
I am the offspring of China.
Once I was the dust of thought,
I dreamed of becoming alive.
I come from a world of respect.
I am made from the dust of my ancestors.
I did not choose to exist.
I won't forget how long I will live.
I see myself falling away as if I were light.

JOEY LAU, 5TH GRADE
CLEVELAND ELEMENTARY, ALAMEDA COUNTY
MARY LOESER, CLASSROOM TEACHER
MAUREEN HURLEY, POET-TEACHER

Culture

I am from China.
A foreign land
where rice paddies adorn
the hills.
Stacks upon stacks of
pools, waters muddied
by a lone worker
who plants the seeds
of future generations.

I am from China.
My ancestors ruled vast
plains of land.
They built their country
up from the ground.

I am from China.
Where the mountains
are shrouded in mystery.
Where rolling thunder
mimics the horses'
hooves pounding against
the land in an
endless yet triumphant beat.

I am from a distant culture;
One I know very little of;
Centuries of ritual, celebration
Lost to me.

Luan Shrivner, 9th grade
Redwood Coast
Montessori High,
Humboldt County
Jay Schrivner, Classroom Teacher
Julie Hochfeld, Poet-Teacher

The Fields of Vietnam

I remember the fields of Vietnam.
I was amazed by the workers.
I look into the past
and the images shatter my mind.
I look like my mother, I am living her past.
I see myself writing in a language
unknown to me.
I have my family by my side.
I come from a different place, nothing like this.
I am made of steel, nothing can hurt me.
From a lazy child to a hard working teenager,
I become a reflection of my mother.
My family comes from Vietnam
Within me is the blood of my ancestors.
I won't forget what they suffered to come here.
No longer shall I disappoint them.

KHLOE PHAN, 5TH GRADE
CLEVELAND ELEMENTARY, ALAMEDA COUNTY
MARY LOESER, CLASSROOM TEACHER
MAUREEN HURLEY, POET-TEACHER

I Come From An Island Adrift in the Pacific

I come from an island
Adrift in the Pacific
Hawaii Nei
Fished from the *kai*
By the *Haoles* and caught
In their net
I am the daughter of immigrants
That come from Cebu
Who paddled their tiny boats
Across the vast, blue sea
Makua kane
A tailor
Makuahine
A goldsmith
The owner of the grocery store downtown
One of the only women that owned a car
The brand new Model T Ford

I was born in March 1918
Born of the sugar cane fields
Of the pineapple plantations
The ocean
The yellow, blue, and black
Diamond-shaped *Humuhumunukunukuapua'a*
And the laid-back *honu*
Gracefully gliding
Through the clear waters

I am the second of twelve *keiki*
Nine girls and three boys
Now fifteen years of age, I've known Poverty

Fear
Fear of going to bed with a hungry belly
Fear of my responsibility
To my family
That the money would soon run out
Fear of a marriage I did not want
Forced upon me
By my 'Ohana
To a stranger
Still just a boy
I do not love him
The name
Brigoli
Still sounds strange on me
I am still a girl myself

But diabetes is a terrible disease
There was a funeral
My father's ashes spread
Along the shoreline
With every wave
More and more gone
Taken from us by Akua
The money dwindled
And my mother could no longer care for me
She thought they had money
She thought I would be well off
But she thought wrong
They are farmers
And now where I live
There is never enough

To go around
Except for hungry bellies
I miss the smells of home
Her cooking
Lumpia, Chicken Adobo, and Pancit
The sounds of my siblings
Playing and quarreling
My sisters
Teasing my brothers
I hope that my sons will be raised well
I wish I could care for them
But I cannot stay
I told Emil
I'm leaving
There are just too many *pukas*
In my life

kai = sea
Haoles = foreigners
Makua kane= father
Makuahine = mother
Humuhumunukunukuapua'a = reef triggerfish
honu = turtle
keiki = children
'Ohana = family
Akua = God
pukas = holes

Ashley Glancy, 9th grade
Lowell High School, San Francisco County
Ms. Carney, Classroom Teacher
Susan Terence, Poet-Teacher

Call Me Chicano

It is 1968.
Six years ago the great Cesar Chavez
Founded the National Farm Workers Association
To push for rights,
Rights not just for the farmworkers
Working day and night to pick the food for your tables—
But rights for all of his people,
My people,
Our people.
Because our people are being segregated in their schools.
Our people are being beat by police officers at protests
For suspicion of disturbing the peace
When all we want is justice.
Our people are being looked down upon
And told that we are not good enough to go to college
So we drop out of high school
Before we even get the chance to prove you wrong.
You see, if you're like us and your skin isn't white
Or your name can't be pronounced without an accent
Or you're what they call "Chicano,"
You're nothing but a number.
A number to add to dropout rates—
Poverty rates,
A number to compare to the white community and claim
That it's not privilege but ethnicity
That determines one's success.
And if you live in Los Angeles?
Forget about it.
It may be called the City of Angels
But it isn't any heaven on Earth.
Because that's where we're worst off.

People like us aren't seen as equals.
No, people like us are beat down—
Punches to the face,
Kicks to the body.
We're seen as inferior,
Dirty,
Worthless.
What about all the people like us working in the fields,
Picking fruit for you dammit?
What about people like us who want to succeed,
Who would if you just gave us a chance?
What about people like me?
I'm not just a number.
I have a name.
And even if you can't pronounce it, I'm no less human.
Go ahead, call me "Chicano,"
You use it as an insult
But I'll take it with pride.
I'll take this word and make it mine,
Because if that's how you label me and my people and my ethnicity,
Then I'll be proud as hell to have it.
People like Cesar Chavez and I have already taken blows to the body,
To our minds,
To our souls,
Why should we let your words be just as painful?

Angelina Leanos, 12th grade
Channel Islands High School, Ventura County
Nicholas Schlesinger, Classroom Teacher
Fernando Salinas, Poet-Teacher

I Am From...

I am from the steamy ships leaving
the deck with a giant splash of worry.

I am from steaming hot Tucson, Arizona
while hot sweat trickles down.

I am from the creek in my backyard
I visit to keep cool.

I am from the cold breath
of nature's call.

I am from school where I meet my friends
as we sing our hearts out.

I am from the quiet house of ghosts lurking around
with their gruesome hearts.

I am from the heavens of fresh water running
down my face after the pool.

I am from the grey cloud where a rain storm
is tearing up.

LILLY LONG, 4TH GRADE
MONTECITO UNION SCHOOL, SANTA BARBARA COUNTY
HEATHER BRUSKI, CLASSROOM TEACHER
CIE GUMUCIO, POET-TEACHER

2 Languages

I get corrected the language I speak
I get made fun of everyday that I talk
Discriminating me makes me feel weak
I have no choice, my mouth has to lock.

2 languages is the key to success
You can talk to many different people
Making mistakes makes you feel over-stressed
But some people make me feel equal.

Yet they stare weird and it's disrespectful
Speaking 2 languages is like 2 lives
Life is hard and it is very regretful
You just have to stay calm and have good vibes.

Speaking two languages is like learning two cultures
You can make life just into 1 sculpture.

RAUL SOTO, 8TH GRADE
HAMILTON PARKWAY SCHOOL, MARIN COUNTY
TANYA MADSEN, CLASSROOM TEACHER
TERRI GLASS, POET-TEACHER

Directions to My Home, My Heart

Go through the mystical creek that lets you feel
    your childhood memories.
Listen to the trees say, "this way."
Look through the spiny bushes
that once had berries.
Look at the dangerous rose that left ashes behind.
Now open the unlocked, chained doors.
Now feel the hurricane winds.
Go left where this wolf will greet you.
There I'll be standing in the forest to dance
and disappear in flames.

BREYANA WRIGHT, 6TH GRADE
JAMES MONROE ELEMENTARY, SONOMA COUNTY
NIKKI WINOVICH, CLASSROOM TEACHER
PHYLLIS MESHULAM, POET-TEACHER

My Hands Are Helpful

My hands can make people turn into chameleons.

My hands can make fruit float.

My hands can make cats appear in a box from a friend.

My hands can help my friends do homework

when they have a hard time.

My hands can make people have good lives.

My hands can shape into animals to escape danger.

My hands will be what I want them to do.

My hands can change color.

My hands can be my future.

JORDAN CASTAÑEDA, 3RD GRADE
DANA GRAY ELEMENTARY, MENDOCINO COUNTY
ERIN SMITH, CLASSROOM TEACHER
KAREN LEWIS, POET-TEACHER

Self Portrait

My hands are tangled steel wires.
My face is a broken mirror.
My eyes are like dark windows to an old house.
My arms are like two sides of a valley.
My legs are like stone pillars that always carry me.
My hair is a forest of dark pines.
My voice is scratchy and tinny, like an old recording.
My boots are like hammers striking the dust.
My soul is welcoming and loving, but old and tired.
My life is confusing as all hell, and my mind is whirling.

BEN SMITH, 12TH GRADE
MADRONE HIGH SCHOOL, MARIN COUNTY
ALEXIS MORGAN, CLASSROOM TEACHER
LEA ASCHKENAS, POET-TEACHER

Perspective

I am whatever you want me to be
The music to your day or
that annoying guy over there.
I was once that,
now I am this.
I could be anything—
a dog
the wind.
I could be faster than lightning
or slower than a sloth.
I am anything to anybody
and anybody could be anything to me
as long as we have perspective
and if we have different points of view
Anybody could be anything to any one

ELI CHARLES GRIFFEN, 4TH GRADE
MENDOCINO K-8 ELEMENTARY, MENDOCINO COUNTY
LINDA FREELING, CLASSROOM TEACHER
HUNTER GAGNON, POET-TEACHER

A Hundred Hairs of a Fox
~Poems About Animals~

I Wonder What the Animals Would Say

I wonder what the animals would say if they could speak....

Would the fox tell us how every minute he lives in constant fear
of being shot and laying on the ground weak?
Is the luxury of a fur coat more important than considering a life;
a life of an innocent creature who was looked up to
by his children and his partner?

And what about the baby calf, the one who was dragged away
from her mother, just days old?
If she wasn't shun to silence, she would share her story.
She would share the fact that she never had a mother to bond with,
but instead lived in negligence
as the industry workers shoved her into a tiny dark stall until she
would soon be impregnated
over and over again for bodily secretions.
She would tell us how she was used and abused for milk that went
to all the babies, but hers.

And what about the pig?
Would the pig tell us he doesn't understand why
the image of bacon comes before his life?
This pig has to be sent off into the middle of nowhere,
and only sees the light once before
entering the area of his slaughter.
The fact that he knows he's treated differently than dogs and cats,
and still nothing is done, is
extremely unjust.

And all this time some of our eyes are still closed.
Some of our minds can't do the right thing;

and this is why some of us need to stand up
and help the rest of US.

ELIYA YAVI, 7TH GRADE
WALTER REED MIDDLE SCHOOL, LOS ANGELES COUNTY
DANIELLE DAGILIS, CLASSROOM TEACHER
JESSICA M. WILSON, POET-TEACHER

It's Raining Rats and Cats

It's raining
It's raining rats and cats
It's raining cats and rats
They splash in puddles
The cats and rats
Rats and cats
The cats chase the rats in the wet, wet, world
The rats chase mice in the wet, wet world
The rats like to swim in the river of gold, and
the cats take flight to escape the endless black hole of water
The cats and rats ride the lightning
The thunder makes an opening for
the rats and cats to swim through
The gray rats, pink rats, green rats,
and blue rats, red rats too,
blue cats, grey cats, yellow cats, green cats,
red cats, pink cats, go to their owners,
new and old,
old or young,
all have a home in the rain.

ROWAN CARR, 3RD GRADE
DANA GRAY ELEMENTARY, MENDOCINO COUNTY
ERIN SMITH, CLASSROOM TEACHER
KAREN LEWIS, POET-TEACHER

Golden Dog

At day, I am a normal child. But at night I am a golden dog. You cannot see me. I am invisible, but I teleport to your house when you have a bad dream or can't go to sleep. Now I will tell you what to do when that happens. If you have a stuffed animal dog, grab it and whisper "Golden Dog, help me and keep me safe during dark times." Then give it a big hug. Have it lie next to you and say "Good night, Golden Dog." I will keep you safe for the night. If you don't have a stuffed animal dog, repeat the process except with a pillow. It might sound weird, but trust me, it will help you so much.

ASHLYNN ORSI, 4TH GRADE
DANA GRAY ELEMENTARY, MENDOCINO COUNTY
JANICE SVERKO, CLASSROOM TEACHER
KAREN LEWIS, POET-TEACHER

Crab

Crawl across the ocean floor
Pinch your meal and gobble it up
Feel the water hit your back
Shimmer red velvet colors on you
Graze in the depths of
deep, deep ocean.

ARMAN ENTEZARI, 2ND GRADE
MONTECITO UNION SCHOOL, SANTA BARBARA COUNTY
HEIDI CRAINE, CLASSROOM TEACHER
LOIS KLEIN, POET-TEACHER

The Great Harris' Hawk

Talons so sharp.
Killing its prey
in one stab.
Flying like a jet
ready to attack
over the desert
at low altitude.

A mouse!
Skills for hunting!
"Wham!"

Lunch is served.

Beak like a knife,
eyes like a camera,
talons as sharp as a
shark's tooth,
wings like a jet!

Thank you,
Oh Mighty Harris' Hawk.

Willis Cardot, 3rd grade
Montecito Union School, Santa Barbara County
Lisa Monson, classroom teacher
Megan Young, Poet-Teacher

A Goodbye Day for the Mosquito Eater

On a sunny day with clouds, rats

    with

        wings

                fly in the

sky and begin hovering over

    jewels and flying

into satellites, then

they

    ran into the

mosquito eater full

of anger. So they

took him to

    the sea anemone.

He couldn't

help so they took

him to the chameleon of

peace, but the chameleon

ate him, and that was the end.

KATELYN BURBECK, 3RD GRADE
DANA GRAY ELEMENTARY, MENDOCINO COUNTY
SUSAN GARRATT, CLASSROOM TEACHER
KAREN LEWIS, POET-TEACHER

Dragons

Dragons come from rain
The rain comes from video games
The video games come from lava
The lava comes from a volcano
The volcano comes from a dead bird
The dead bird comes from a hunter
The hunter comes from a wolf
The wolf comes from pizza
The pizza comes from Star Wars
Star Wars comes from TV
TV comes from mummies
Mummies come from super glue
Super glue comes from teeth
Teeth come from Legos
Legos comes from me

LEIF SWENSON, 3RD GRADE
DELPHI ACADEMY, LOS ANGELES COUNTY
ANN SWAPP, CLASSROOM TEACHER
ALICE PERO, POET-TEACHER

Animals in the Jungle

The parrot cries
The blue morpho flies
The anaconda lies
In the jungle

The soil thrives crops
The river, the dolphin mops
The kakapo hops
In the jungle

The tree frog flips
Through the river floats the ships
The piranha nips
In the jungle

The pheasant clucks
The okapi bucks
The explorer's animal rescue trucks
In the jungle

All things are beautiful in the jungle.

RONAN CORBIT, 3RD GRADE
STRAWBERRY POINT SCHOOL, MARIN COUNTY
KRISTINA PUTALIK, CLASSROOM TEACHER
TERRI GLASS, POET-TEACHER

Bald Eagle Rap

Eagles been hiding from the tension on the rise
Bald Eagles must be careful when they fly
The people hunt them from below
And they just don't know
That there aren't many Eagles left alive

Above rivers and streams
I perch and I wait for the fish to swim by
Not noticing when I fly
Straight for its back
And I grab with razor sharp talons
My hooked beak displays more of my talents!
I tear and rip and shred fish to pieces
Then I fly home to go feed my babies

As long as a stream or a river is nearby
Fish and other small animals maintain my food supply
I take what I need, but not more than that
Four to five weeks until my family gets fat!
Thriving, not surviving is where I want to be
I will ensure the future of my family

I can eat anything really
Living or dead
I'd prefer fish over invertebrates
Other birds, rabbits, and muskrats are fine
Salmon is my favorite dish upon to dine
I eat lizards and bugs, and they are okay
As soon as they see me

They quickly dash away
I chase them even though they're quicker and faster than me
But I take what I can get
When I have gone for weeks.

JAMAL HEWITT, 3RD GRADE
WILLOW CREEK ACADEMY, MARIN COUNTY
ANNE SISKIN & CHRIS GOMES, CLASSROOM TEACHERS
LINDEN BERRY, POET-TEACHER

Tiger's Breath & Dragons

Find me in the sparkling moonlight
in the shimmering bay of San Francisco
Hear me in the fall when the fluttering leaves
fall to the rigid ground
Feel me in the warmth of a tiger's breath,
where I come from,
where golden and red dragons dance around
for Chinese New Year
Feel me in nature when the roots
of the tall Sequoia trees
touch the fiery hot core of the Earth
Find me in the CN Tower
where the speeding elevators
whoosh
like the hummingbirds of America

RAFFERTY KAN, 3RD GRADE
STRAWBERRY POINT ELEMENTARY, MARIN COUNTY
CRISTI MCCABE, CLASSROOM TEACHER
PRARTHO SERENO, POET-TEACHER

Crow

me.
an ugly black crow
somehow in a jungle-like forest.

All the other birds think,
"What an ugly parrot!"

They do not care
that they are talking instead of
whispering.

but, i don't care.

I don't care that some birds look like
they are encrusted with gold or
rubies or that their feathers resemble
dusk.

All I want is to be beautiful.

Is that too much to ask for?

Why can't they say, "She is one very
blessed crow?"

"Wait, no."
I want more than anything not to be
a crow.

So, as I stare among the trees,
the willow trees,

I ask, "Why?"

When all the birds of beautiful colors
leave me behind.

"Why?"

Charlee Cate Cardot, 4th grade
Montecito Union School, Santa Barbara County
Raina Mather, Classroom Teacher
Cie Gumucio, Poet-Teacher

Spring Wolf

Redwood trees cover the woods
wolf pups run wild like the leaves
as they fall to the ground

Watching warms your heart—
a mother's love shines in her eyes
as she watches her pup, a runty little pup

When I am here watching this, my blood warms
As night falls, a blood moon rises
every wolf howls as loud as a child's scream

As night comes to end, another life starts
around the river bend, when a wolf pup
howls along

KYLIE LUNA, 4TH GRADE
CERRA VISTA ELEMENTARY SCHOOL, SAN BENITO COUNTY
GABRIELA VALLEJO, CLASSROOM TEACHER
AMANDA CHIADO, POET-TEACHER

Ocelot

Spots to blend in, dark as the night,

Paws to run, hiding from sight,

Whiskers to feel, claws to scratch,

Ears hear fear, teeth to catch,

Clean with a tongue, legs to move,

Tails to whip, fur with grooves,

Eyes dart around, haunches tucked in,

Claws on paws, catching some mice

Swimming with grace

I'm an ocelot.

Jude Park, 5th grade
Park School, Marin County
Andrea Dunn, Classroom Teacher
Claire Blotter, Poet-Teacher

Gorillas

I roll around on the nice soft grass
Then I yell out ooo ee ehh—that means
that they need to come back.
They come running back.
I am the leader, the silverback.
I hear a baby gorilla yell ooo ehh ehh—
that means help, it keeps yelling.
I get closer every second.
Finally, I see a jaguar growling at the gorilla.
I barge in, knocking the jaguar out of the way
pounding it with my fists, then killing it.
The baby is safe, we go back to the group.
The mom and the baby are safe, together.
It is night. I hear someone coming, humans!
Suddenly, something is wrapped around my neck
then everything goes black.

YAMILA ESPER, 5TH GRADE
PRESTWOOD ELEMENTARY, SONOMA COUNTY
RHONDA PIPKIN, CLASSROOM TEACHER
SANDRA ANFANG, POET-TEACHER

The Snowdrift Penguin

Sleek, slide, swim
This is the Arctic
Black, gray, white
This is the Arctic
From fluffy down to slippery feathers
The penguin dives to catch food
Salty fish is a delicacy
To all the snow dwellers
It tastes of juicy salt water
Cold as ice
The freezing snow drifts feel like powder
Soft as a blanket
The calling penguin sounds like a strong cry
Loud as a siren
The rising sun looks like a glowing orb
Bright as honey
The summer wind smells like fresh leaves
Sweet as pollen
Penguins notice everything

ALI POST, 5TH GRADE
PARK SCHOOL, MARIN COUNTY
ANDREA DUNN, CLASSROOM TEACHER
CLAIRE BLOTTER, POET-TEACHER

El Oso

El oso es color café,
y come carne,
y es grande,
y pesa mucho.
El oso tiene uñas grandes
y ataca su presa sin pensarlo,
y es muy peligroso,
y duerme en montañas.
Y eso
es todo
lo que sé del oso.

The Bear

The bear is brown
and eats meat
and is huge
and weighs a lot.
The bear has big claws
and attacks his prey easily
and is very dangerous
and sleeps in the mountains.
And this
is all
that I know about the bear.

ADÁN BAQUIAX, 5TH GRADE
SAN PEDRO ELEMENTARY, MARIN COUNTY
CASSIE LANE, CLASSROOM TEACHER
LEA ASCHKENAS, POET-TEACHER / TRANSLATOR

The Bandit

I am a bandit, a villain.
I rob,
I scavenge.
I am a raccoon.
I wear the rings I've stolen,
around my tail,
made not of gold or silver,
but of the darkness of the night,
the darkness of my heart.

They categorize me,
as the great unknown,
the danger,
the evil,
The enemy of the light.
Some think my heart is good,
they try to love me,
they try to fix me,

Ha.
They don't know me at all.

I save my words,
and speak to scare,
to frighten,
to harm.
Unless I'm being run over by a car.
Still...
I watch,
I hate,
I envy,

The beauty of the heron,
the bravery of the tiger,
the charm of the dolphin,
the peculiarity of the cow,
the strength of the bear,
and me.
The liar.
The outcast.
The fool.
I am not ashamed,
rather,
angry.
But I am sly,
I am witty,
yet I am not pretty.
I am a cruel,
yet proud,
Bandit.

ISABELLA SCHLITT, 5TH GRADE
WEST MARIN SCHOOL, MARIN COUNTY
ESTHER UNDERWOOD, CLASSROOM TEACHER
BRIAN KIRVEN, POET-TEACHER

Bird

Oh volcano junco you are
mysterious like a ghost
you are like fire
inside the gut.

you fly like an angel
but better

you have long feathers like
hair your feet are
thin and weak like sticks

your eyes are yellow
like an owl

you're like a ghost
you suck the spirit
out of people you go
deep and become them.

you're the king of
the realm but evil

you touch so lightly
it hurts

I spy with my little eye
you eating worms taking
their lives

you live in a volcano

hot yet cold you live
forever and never die

I wish you were me
I admire your darkness
I imagine your evil

Thank you for being
ALIVE.

Rosie Murray, 5th grade
Adams School, Santa Barbara County
Mrs. Chalmers, Classroom Teacher,
Lalli Dana Drobny, Poet-Teacher

Smoke of the Wind

I see a fox approaching me.
Its fur looks black, blows in the wind.
It no longer smells like lavender but
a smoky smell.
I can sense the pain in its eyes
of watching its home burn to the ground,
and how this fox protects me.
It's my turn.
I suddenly get bombarded with visions
of people trying to start more of the things
that caused my fox to have pain and
smell like smoke.
I know what I have to do. As I realize this,
its pain fades—never completely—
but enough so I can see a sparkle.
As it fades into the shadows,
its smoky smell catches the wind and
it makes me sad, but that lavender smell
will come back. Its eyes will go back to that bright blue,
and its fur to silver, no longer
covered in the ashes of its home.

Ava Baldwin Ferguson, 6th grade
James Monroe Elementary, Sonoma County
Nikki Winovich, Classroom Teacher
Phyllis Meshulam, Poet-Teacher

The Fox

Fox, Fox
Why are you so cute?

Heaven gave me a cute face from above.

Fox, Fox
Can I call you Flower?

Of course, just call me Blossom not Flower.

Fox, Fox
How are you so smart?

I know tricks of my own not telling one single word.

JUDITH PINA, 5TH GRADE
LEONORA FILLMORE ELEMENTARY SCHOOL, SANTA BARBARA COUNTY
AMY WILSON, CLASSROOM TEACHER
MICHELLE PITTENGER, POET-TEACHER

Dear Wolf

Dear Wolf, in white and black,
I have some questions I must ask.
What are these questions?

Dear Wolf, oh so sly.
Why must you howl at the night sky?
It was a job given by the sky.

Dear Wolf, full of beauty,
Why do your eyes shine like rubies?
It was a gift from the ground, who is usually moody.

Dear Wolf, I must go. Hopefully, I'll see you tomorrow.
May you not know sorrow.

Amirah McGee, 5th grade
Leonora Fillmore Elementary School, Santa Barbara County
Amy Wilson, Classroom teacher
Michelle Pittenger, Poet-teacher

The Life of a Cat

I am just a cat
I don't understand why that person I live with
always pokes me when I'm trying to sleep
Why do they always ask me things as if I'm listening
Why do other people say I'm "so cute!" and try to pet me,
but I just run and hide so I don't
have to put up with them.
Why does my owner feed me so much and make me so fat
Why don't they want me jumping on the
table to share their food
Why can't I just sit in my box in peace
without them taking so many pictures?

JASMINE MORTON, 6TH GRADE
COASTAL GROVE CHARTER SCHOOL, HUMBOLDT COUNTY
JENNY RUSHBY, CLASSROOM TEACHER
JULIE HOCHFELD, POET-TEACHER

Happiness

I see you, beautiful blue dolphin,
I won't harm you.
"Come here!!"
I don't feel like
you're going to harm me.
I feel protected when I'm with you.
Your eyes are
as beautiful
as stars. I don't feel pain
when I'm with
you. I feel relieved.
I can be me
without judgment.
Lead me through
my pain; be my
sunshine to my darkness
You're full of happiness
and love.
You came in my life
& changed it. You're full of joy.

Amy Arenal, 6th grade
James Monroe Elementary School, Sonoma County
Nikki Winovich, Classroom Teacher
Phyllis Meshulam, Poet-Teacher

Phoenix

I see you with your ruby-like eyes.

With your amber feathers,

circling my fingers like harmless fire.

You fly quickly and swiftly, your eyes

glinting like fireworks.

You gave me past

and hope for the future. Bright, bright,

is your welcoming sun.

You fly away, feathers high. Burst into flame.

You fade away.

Your burned ashes carry your cinnamon scent.

Come to me again.

Take me back to your spiritual world.

Let me rest in your aura.

ARISBET CAMACHO, 6TH GRADE
JAMES MONROE ELEMENTARY, SONOMA COUNTY
NIKKI WINOVICH, CLASSROOM TEACHER
PHYLLIS MESHULAM, POET-TEACHER

Pegasus

I see you in the sky
looking down at me.
Tell me about you a little bit.
When I'm in the forest, where
there's just a clearing,
there are no trees there.
I look into the distance and I see you
but I don't know who you are or
what you are. And then I see
you have wings, and then you start leaving.
Come to me, please, come to me.
What is your secret? Will I see you again?
You are white, with shining eyes,
ready to tell me something.
Please come back to me. Come back to me.
Please tell me your secret.
"I am an animal. I came down to see you.
One cool fact about me is that
I am the symbol of poetry."
Will I see you again?
"Sure. Just close your eyes and think about me.
And I will come back to this same spot."

Joshua Gomez, 6th grade
Abraham Lincoln Elementary School, Sonoma County
Tawni Johnson, Classroom Teacher
Phyllis Meshulam, Poet-Teacher

I See You

I see you, cat, by a purple glow
of a clear night sky, by the galaxy,
your glowing blue diamond eyes.
Your mysterious soft meow chills up the night.
Your black and white fur
is like the future of the solar system.
Your tail feels like it stops time.
Nothing less than your purr shines with
the moonlight, a blue flame covers
your eye like a whisper inside.
I'll call you Shadow. Eyes are closed.
Stars collide. Let's enjoy this mysterious night.

ERIC DOMINGUEZ, 6TH GRADE
JAMES MONROE ELEMENTARY, SONOMA COUNTY
MIKE PERSINGER, CLASSROOM TEACHER
PHYLLIS MESHULAM, POET-TEACHER

Winter

Deep in a warm cozy home
A little kitten sits by a fire
Snuggling against a stand still gnome
Dreaming of its small little desire
A cup of warm milk fizzy with foam
Spilling over a gorgeous cup to admire

While outside lies a fox frigid with cold
Looking through the foggy window
Wishing it had a coat colored with gold
To fight against the freezing white snow.

Genevive Briceno, 6th grade
Hamilton School, Glenn County
Jon Anger, Classroom Teacher
Terri Glass, Poet-Teacher

INFINITY IS THE NAME
OF MY SOUL

Infinity

Inside my soul is the door to tomorrow,
a gateway to paradise,
a wardrobe to empty air.
My soul is a stream that goes on forever,
and a piercing scream.
My soul is a totem pole
rising as far as I can see.
Infinity is the name of my soul.

DONOVAN TOPETE ALVARADO, 5TH GRADE
LU SUTTON, MARIN COUNTY
MRS. HINXMANN, CLASSROOM TEACHER
TERRI GLASS, POET-TEACHER

You Are Mine

You are a spider weaving a home for writing
You are a blooming flower brightening up my day
You are a flute singing a lovely song to me
You are the sunshine after rain
You are a sewing machine that sews us
      back together when we are apart

Savina Hamm, 2nd grade
Montecito Union School, Santa Barbara County
Jacki Hammer, Classroom Teacher
Lois Klein, Poet-Teacher

Let It Live

Let the blossoms bloom
Let the bells ring
Those are some
signs that I know
it is spring.
A kid like me
still waiting
for the animals to
stop hibernating.
Those are the reasons
it is almost spring
Blossoms raining on me
and me sprinting though
them enjoying a decade-
old life. I'm not afraid
to jump into a lake.
I let the warm bottom
of the lake touch my
freezing toes.
No, no more snow
Yes, yes colorful
dresses. I ride my
bike giving a smile to
every neighbor,
strangers, bugs,
plants, even a
tiny ant because
I got spring
fever. I have
a contagious
case it's called

happiness and
it's taken over
my body.
To the plants,
to the ants,
to myself,
I say
Let it Live.

Maya Huizar, 4th grade
Poinsettia Elementary, Ventura County
Diane Sather and Julie Soske, Classroom Teachers
Jennifer Kelley, Poet-Teacher

When I Listen

When I listen closely,
I can hear the world *buzzing*
around me

little bees *swarming* in flower patches
trying to get pollen to make honey

like birds *chirping* in the rainforest,
communicating

like a *booming* waterfall,
crashing down a mountain

an opera singer, her voice
mesmerizing the crowd

the soothing *pitter patter* of rain

enormous waves *crashing* on the shore,
like little froggies *croaking*

like a wolf, *howling* at the moon

like a poet, a whole loud world
in their mind

hummingbirds *buzzing*,
robots *beeping*,
musicians *playing*,
bears *snoring*

the *whoosh* of a baseball being hit,
the *clopping* of a horse on pavement

This is what I hear
when I listen

Josie Morris, 4th grade
Vieja Valley Elementary, Santa Barbara County
Tairy Birkley, Classroom Teacher
Cie Gumucio, Poet-Teacher

Most Beautiful

The most unique thing is my
  mind popping with ideas.
The strangest thing I ever saw was
  other people thinking,
with their elbows smack on the table and their pencils
  moving like cheetahs.
The most beautiful thing is the stars
  looking down on me.

The brightest thing I ever saw was
  a unicorn dancing in the sun.
The most colorful thing I ever saw was a rainbow in
  the bright blue sky.
The warmest thing I ever felt was my kitty's heart
  pounding with love.
The most beautiful thing I ever saw was the world
  spinning and spinning.
The sweetest thing I ever saw was my family
  looking into my heart...
But I will never know what they are thinking.

BLOOMA GOLDBERG, 3RD GRADE
PARK SCHOOL, MARIN COUNTY
JULIE HERRARA, CLASSROOM TEACHER
PRARTHO SERENO, POET-TEACHER

La Felicidad

La felicidad es mi familia.
La felicidad es el color azul.
Mi felicidad es la escuela.
Mi felicidad es estar con mis amigos.
La felicidad es compartir.
Felicidad es hacer la tarea bien.
Felicidad es salir a jugar.
La felicidad es como el helado.
La felicidad es estar con mi maestra.
Mi felicidad es el equipo de futbol.
La felicidad de otros es muy buena.
La felicidad es de todos.

Happiness

Happiness is my family.
Happiness is the color blue.
Happiness is school.
My happiness is being with my friends.
Happiness is sharing.
Happiness is doing a good job on homework.
Happiness is going out to play.
Happiness is like ice-cream.
Happiness is being with my teacher.
My happiness is a soccer team.
The happiness of others is good.
Happiness is for everyone.

Brayan Camay, 5th grade
Olive Elementary, Marin County
Fran Rozoff, Classroom Teacher
Lea Aschkenas, Poet-Teacher /
Translator

Portrait of Joy

Joy is a tall, bright happy man. He walks around with his cane. He always gives the warmest greetings. Joy has the calmest dog ever while he, on the other hand, is filled with energy. He gives food to the homeless and always goes doorstep to doorstep handing out newspapers. Sometimes his trench coat gets stuck on the doorknobs or he drops his cane, but he just laughs. He smells like pollen and he feels like flowers. Everywhere he goes, the sun is shining.

RYAN MARTIN, 5TH GRADE
BROOKS ELEMENTARY SCHOOL, SONOMA COUNTY
SARA AIRES, CLASSROOM TEACHER
JACKIE HUSS HALLERBERG, POET-TEACHER

Gracefulness

Gracefulness is like the morning sun shining upon you.
Gracefulness can soar through space.
It can be a deer grazing on life that has had its chance.
Gracefulness is everything that can be possible.
Its smooth barrier is protecting it from anger and hate.
Gracefulness can do anything it wants.
It can never be broken.
Its closest friends are Happy and Sad, the opposites.
Gracefulness is life. Like stars and the moon shining again.
Gracefulness is life. Everywhere.
Deer grazing on life. Everywhere life
has had its chance. Everywhere, anywhere.
Life.

ALICE JOHNSON, 3RD GRADE
LOMA VERDE SCHOOL, MARIN COUNTY
KAREN MCCORMISH, CLASSROOM TEACHER
CLAIRE BLOTTER, POET-TEACHER

Wonder

The deepest hole is full of darkness,
a touch of light can lift your brightness.

The easiest thing is to lose your truth,
but if you do, what will become of you?

The wrinkliest time is the tick of the tock,
the weight of lies is on the top.

The smoothest river, so heavy and light,
the touch of whispers in the night.

The happiest whisper, just one whisper,
can make your happiness rise.

XOANA ZAMUDIO-TRUNCOS, 4TH GRADE
EDNA MAGUIRE SCHOOL, MARIN COUNTY
ANN ESHOFF, CLASSROOM TEACHER
PRARTHO SERENO, POET-TEACHER

Courage

Standing up to enemies, COURAGE

Attempting a challenge course, COURAGE, littered with obstacles

COURAGE, running for a high office in government

Taking a stand for what you believe in, COURAGE

COURAGE, helping a friend when they needed it

Protecting others, COURAGE, and risking getting hurt

Going on long journeys across deserts and oceans, COURAGE

Going through battlefields, COURAGE, and smelling the pain & suffering

COURAGE, to answer that incredibly hard question

Taking control of a dangerous situation, COURAGE

Having a disability, COURAGE, but powering through

COURAGE, helping others to help them believe that they can do anything.

Adam Gelfand, 5th grade
Strawberry Point Elementary, Marin County
Danny Gasparini, Classroom Teacher
Terri Glass, Poet-Teacher

I Believe in the Wind

I believe in the wind.

I believe that I have strength when my
Cherokee ancestors call to me.

I believe in the ocean that comes together
with the wind and guides my sail to a new direction.

I believe in the sweet soil and dirt I stand upon.

I believe in the music that rings in my ears and makes me
dance and scream that life just isn't what it seems.

I believe in the warmth in a fire that tells
me I'm safe.

I believe in the feet I move to go to every
place and maybe even to space!

I believe in my dreams I dream and the perfect
detailed streams of my imagination.

I believe in life and death and whatever's in between.

I believe in sadness, I believe in madness, and I
believe in happiness.

But what I don't believe in is the fear and lump in my
throat when I need to speak up
                    for the ones that I
        love.... Even me.

Oh I believe in the wind.

JAIDA STEINEBAUGH, 6TH GRADE
MCKINLEYVILLE MIDDLE SCHOOL, HUMBOLDT COUNTY
MARCY HOWE, CLASSROOM TEACHER
DAN ZEV LEVINSON, POET-TEACHER

Free

It was a dark night,
it looked like a piece of tar
all over the night..
the night like a mystery.

WHOOSH…
the wind swipes me away.

CRASH… I land on the moon,
in a dusty cloud.

I stand up.

SWISH… I jump as high as a
mountain.

I hear no sound except the sound of
my feet, *thump, thump, thump.*

My heart beats, but if I listen carefully,
I can hear a car *zooming* by and as
soon as it is gone... *"Dink!"*

I am back on earth, in my house, the
sink goes, *Tap, tap, tap.*

I'm back in my cage, back where
I am supposed to belong,

I belong on the moon, not here.

I want to be free.

Margaret Eglin, 4th grade
Montecito Union School, Santa Barbara County
Heather Bruski, Classroom Teacher
Cie Gumucio, Poet-Teacher

Balloons

A Birthday
every day
would not
be so bad.
Except when
you hear
the sound
of popping balloons.

ANJALI BOSE, 2ND GRADE
NEW ROADS SCHOOL, LOS ANGELES COUNTY
JENNIFER CARTER, CLASSROOM TEACHER
INDIA RADFAR, POET-TEACHER

Me Haces Volar

Tu me haces volar
con tanto amor que
me das

Tu olor me hace
Brillar y mi corazón
empiesa a palpitar

Cuando estoy con
Tigo me pongo
a cantar porque
con tu amore me
haces bailar

You Make Me Fly

You make me fly
with all that love
you've given me

Your scent makes
me shine and my heart
begins to pound

When I'm with you
I raise my voice
to sing because
your love
makes me dance

DARYHAN CARDOZO, 5TH GRADE
HOLLISTER ELEMENTARY SCHOOL,
SANTA BARBARA COUNTY
HUGH RANSON, CLASSROOM TEACHER
RON ALEXANDER, POET-TEACHER

More To The Heart

My heart changes when it chooses.
My heart is what it wants to be.
My heart is the color of a sweet juicy orange.
But there's more to my heart
that I haven't discovered.
From the doors inside it,
opening up each feeling...
Which one is which, I want to know.
I search endlessly, never finding the sunshine.
And seeing the darkness of the moon inside it.
I thought I loved my heart,
I thought I loved everything.
But now I see the world
doesn't revolve around me.
It may be sweet as an orange,
but don't judge a book by its cover.

ISAAC PIÑON, 5TH GRADE
CLEVELAND ELEMENTARY, ALAMEDA COUNTY
MARY LOESER, CLASSROOM TEACHER
MAUREEN HURLEY, POET-TEACHER

In the Heart of Myself

The soaring sky
taught me how to
shine deep in others'
souls.

The golden raindrops
taught me how
to sink in some-
one's heart.

The silver sea
taught the galaxy
how to soar
through the
curtains in the house.

The golden blossom
has secrets to tell you:
how to glow deep
in the world.

In the heart
of myself
I see a glow
of hope

I hear a star
whispering
in my soul

And I feel

a rush of
pride gliding
beside me.

SHENGXI HUANG, 3RD GRADE
FRANCIS SCOTT KEY ELEMENTARY SCHOOL
SAN FRANCISCO COUNTY
CHARISSA LING, CLASSROOM TEACHER
SUSAN TERENCE, POET-TEACHER

Back In Balance

In fall, there is just enough day and night.
But in winter, there is too much night, dark as ink,
and not enough day, as bright as the sky.
I have too little play-time in the day
because night is always right around the corner.
My family has too much work,
even though my mom doesn't have a job.
My neighborhood has too few children outside
as video games take up everyone's time.
The world has too many people,
all living in the tiny earth.
To put things back in balance,
I would make sure everyone has enough,
not too much or too little.

TIGER HAN, 3RD GRADE
SPRECKELS ELEMENTARY, SAN DIEGO COUNTY
DERON BEAR, CLASSROOM TEACHER
CELIA SIGMON, POET-TEACHER

Goddesses Have To Eat Too

If I were a Goddess,
I would make the oceans
out of nacho cheese

the land out of tortilla chips,
& all the people out of
semi-sweet chocolate melts

telephone wires
would be made of Red Vines

cotton candy, for the trees

pumpkin pie houses
lemon cars
tomato mountains
pizza schools

then,
oh, then,

I would eat it all up!

MARGARET FARLEY, 3RD GRADE
EMERYVILLE CENTER OF COMMUNITY LIFE, ALAMEDA COUNTY
SUMMER DAYCARE RESIDENCY
BRENNAN DEFRISCO, POET-TEACHER

Angels in the Sky

Angels help when you need them.
As wars end, you know they're near.
Every time an angel helps,
a new angel is born and grows up in the sky.
We see them as stars.

Angels will love you if you love them,
but if you don't, the sun may disappear.
They are peaceful if you are and
will help you, only if you believe in them.

An Angel's love is a warm feeling.
You can taste clouds and hear the sound
of a clear bell. When it happens
you'll hear an angel say, *I'm here with you.*

These special ones were once humans,
born from the grave into angels.
During wars they are born on tall ships at sea.
An enormous lady in a blue robe receives them.

No one knows where angels come from,
but if you dare ask, I'll tell you—every century
they become leaders of the brightest stars.

And what about the lady in blue? I've heard
she has a mysterious gift, but no one
knows what it is.

When the end
of the earth is near, she'll be there.

You'll smell the fierce sea, sense the storm,
and see her rising from the waves.

Pria Kussat, 3rd grade
Spreckels Elementary School, San Diego County
Deron Bear, Classroom Teacher
Seretta Martin, Poet-Teacher

The Angel with a Mustache

Well... it was an angel and she had blue and pink hair and it reflected. She had a star on her face and blue eyes and a white dress. She had golden shoes and she had a... mustache!!! You didn't see that coming, did you? She also had wings and pink tights and she lives in Canada and sometimes she visits her cousin in Brazil and she can fly to Australia and to Mexico and her name is Chloe and she has a BFF named "Red Girl." She is a devil. So that is my story.

Natalia Stafford, 3rd grade
Delphi Academy, Los Angeles County
Ann Swapp, Classroom Teacher
Alice Pero, Poet-Teacher

The Voice

I believe that the voice of freedom
can change the life of a hopeless
widow. I believe that the voice
of a red rose can silence a
suicidal mindset. I believe that
the voice of two caring classmates
can destroy depression.
I believe that the voice of
judgment will stop darkness in
its path. I believe that the
voice of the reaper is scary and
cold. But what I believe most
is that the voices of the people
we see when we die will cheer
up the sadness of death.

CAMERON HUFFMAN, 7TH GRADE
NORTH COAST LEARNING ACADEMY, HUMBOLDT COUNTY
LISA PAYTON AND REBEKAH DAVIS, CLASSROOM TEACHERS
DAN ZEV LEVINSON, POET-TEACHER

My Secret Place

My secret place is full of cliffs
   and loud waterfalls.
I run across a creek and splash
   in the creek, *thump, thump.*
In the secret place I see a bear cub
   eating honey.
I swim in the river and dry off with a leaf.
The secret place has a vast ocean
   and a large jungle.
I run on the side of the cliff and
   run my hand through a waterfall,
whoooosh.
I dig a burrow at night for warmth
   and sleep on leaves.
In the morning I run along the ocean.
I climb a large tree to see everything.
This is my secret place and I love it.

JACK CONWAY, 3RD GRADE
PRESTWOOD ELEMENTARY, SONOMA COUNTY
CARLY COSTELLO, CLASSROOM TEACHER
SANDRA ANFANG, POET-TEACHER

On the Other Side of Tomorrow

On the other side of tomorrow,
maybe things will be better.

On the other side of tomorrow,
maybe they'll have a cure for it.

On the other side of tomorrow,
maybe there will be another hope.

On the other side of tomorrow,
maybe I'll get lucky.

On the other side of tomorrow,
maybe it will be a perfect day.

On the other side of tomorrow,
maybe it will be like a dream.

On the other side of tomorrow,
maybe something special will happen.

On the other side of tomorrow,
maybe I'll get my greatest wish.

On the other said of tomorrow,
maybe hate and jealousy will take a day off.

AIDAN HURSH, 5TH GRADE
BROOKS ELEMENTARY SCHOOL
SARA AIRES, CLASSROOM TEACHER
JACKIE HALLERBERG, POET-TEACHER

Change

Will people accept me for me?
is a question I ask myself all the time.
I feel like no one will, but then
I think not of that and ask myself
if I will ever change for someone.
No or yes?
This is the one question I cannot answer
because it is the question
nobody has an answer to.
Change is the one thing I will not do
for anyone, so if you don't like me
for me, then just think about this:
"a pretty face is nothing if you have
an ugly heart."

ROSIE McWHORTER, 5TH GRADE
PRESTWOOD ELEMENTARY, SONOMA COUNTY
MRS. PIPKIN, CLASSROOM TEACHER
SANDRA ANFANG, POET-TEACHER

Fire in the Savannah (Dream Poem)

Under the sun of the Savannah it felt
like a bonfire but it was a bonfire.
I saw the hot sparks a few feet in front of me.
I ran and ran.
I got to a burned-up town.
All I wanted was to go back home,
but now I couldn't.
I found a banjo and two pieces of pottery.
As I walked I lost one.
I walked forever. I came to a desert.
I looked up at the sky.
I remembered the stories of kids who lost
their mom and dad.
They say they see a face in the moon and
they never wake up after that.
The last time I saw myself alive
I said, "Now we lift our forces."

ALYSSA HUGHES, 5TH GRADE
PRESTWOOD ELEMENTARY, SONOMA COUNTY
RHONDA PIPKIN, CLASSROOM TEACHER
SANDRA ANFANG, POET-TEACHER

Dying Heart

My heart is beating,
pumping blood throughout my body,
to my brain, to my arms,
legs, torso, like a car pumping
fluids throughout the machine, the
engine, the brakes, the AC, to evolve.
My heart pumps fast, crashes and flashing
lights, sirens are going off.
While I sleep, my heart is climbing
mountains and mountains of a neon green,
hills every second. My heart stops
climbing to enjoy a sweet
relief of a flat field. Bury me
in that green field without a box.
Bury me to power other hearts
of animals and plants.

NOAH SWANSON, 6TH GRADE
MCKINLEYVILLE MIDDLE SCHOOL, HUMBOLDT COUNTY
MARCY HOWE, CLASSROOM TEACHER
DAN ZEV LEVINSON, POET-TEACHER

Lazy Sunday

Today is my favorite day, and I ain't
going out to play, for today I
will ooze, I will snooze, I will saunter away.
I come back from a comic book day.

Come on, let's remember, reflect,
and restore this lazy Sunday. That's why
this is my favorite day.

LEO BEACH, 4TH GRADE
CLAIRE LILIENTHAL SCHOOL, SAN FRANCISCO COUNTY
MS. CARILLO, CLASSROOM TEACHER
GAIL NEWMAN, POET-TEACHER

Calm

I love being calm
like a butterfly in a green valley
where I can do what I want. It feels free.

I gave a sandwich to a homeless man
and I'm not sure what I felt
but it wasn't calm.

People are not always calm.
Sometimes I wish I could
spread what I feel to everyone,

but I think
the homeless person
at least, felt thankful.

Seagrin Lawless, 3rd grade
Spreckels Elementary School, San Diego County
Elizabeth Stewart, Classroom Teacher
Seretta Martin, Poet-Teacher

To Be the Change

Take 2 cups of bravery.
Put 2 tablespoons of heroism in a large container.
Mix with your hands until it's sifted through.
Pour in a cup of intelligence.
Cook in a pan seared with urgency at 100° F. for 100 seconds
until you can feel the change inside of you.

You can tell when it's done by tasting it.
Let cool until it radiates power.
Add a sprinkle of hope.
Slice it up.
Serve it to all the people of the world
one sliver at a time.

PEARL MCKAY, 5TH GRADE
APPLE BLOSSOM SCHOOL, SONOMA COUNTY
DYLAN LICCIARDO, CLASSROOM TEACHER
JACKIE HUSS HALLERBERG, POET-TEACHER

Changes

The tissue turns into a hat and flies away in the wind
and lands in the ocean then turns into a dolphin
and leaps in the air then gets to land and turns back
into a tissue box.

The desk turns into a butterfly and flies away to a cave
and turns into a bear then goes to sleep and becomes
a desk again.

The moon rises up and turns into a giant hawk
then flies down to the water and becomes a fish
then turns into the moon again.

A shooting star comes down to earth
then turns into a dove and flies to a tree
and turns into a hat and flies into a house
and turns back into a star.

Hazel Dale, 3rd grade
Delphi Academy, Los Angeles County
Grant Youn, Classroom Teacher
Alice Pero, Poet-Teacher

Mad Hatter

Purple green red orange
a blue dress a cat
a kettle a hat
a rabbit a girl a thing
I want to hurl
Humpty Dumpty sat on a wall
I just want to drink it all
tea hee hee
wee wee wee
a queen a lass
through the looking glass
a time a place
let's have a party
let's drink some tea
come Alice
pass me that chalice
a tree
oh look there's a bee
the caterpillar huffs and puffs
Clubs
Spades
Diamonds
and Hearts Hearts Hearts.

WYATT KENNEDY, 10TH GRADE
REDWOOD HIGH SCHOOL, MARIN COUNTY
JENNIFER MADDEN, CLASSROOM TEACHER
CLAIRE BLOTTER, POET-TEACHER

Tomorrow

Tomorrow I will have eggs for breakfast
Tomorrow is a curtain I haven't looked behind
Tomorrow I plan to do nothing
Tomorrow I will sleep in
Tomorrow is another day and another dusk
Tomorrow is a mountain that has not been climbed
Tomorrow the bees will make honey
Tomorrow the wasps will still sting
Tomorrow I will hide inside from my allergies
Tomorrow I sleep, but today, I party
Tomorrow's yesterday is today
Tomorrow is tomorrow's tomorrow

Caitlin O'Donnell, Teagan Petric,
Cesar Jarquin Flores, Alesio Riggs, Baylen Feyh,
6th grade Summer Workshop, Sonoma County
Torina Feyh, Workshop Coordinator
Brennan DeFrisco, Poet-teacher

I Don't Know

I don't know what's inside of me but every
second I feel like it's snowing outside
and I'm inside with my friends
and family sipping heated cocoa and
watching a nice movie it's
like a fair with fun rides and
candy floss and mini donuts it feels
like a burning summer day at
camp it's like a sleepover
with your best friend doing your
favorite things it's like the end of
school activities it's like a birthday
pie it's like when you actually get
math it's sledding down a snowy hill
it's anything but bad.

PHAEDRA STEADMAN, 4TH GRADE
WHITETHORN ELEMENTARY SCHOOL, HUMBOLDT COUNTY
ELIZABETH BALLOU, CLASSROOM TEACHER
DAN ZEV LEVINSON, POET-TEACHER

My World

In my world there is more love, less hate

In my own world, each puppy has a loving owner

In my world there is world peace and happiness

In this world is my hope

my soul

my life

NADYA BRODETSKY, 4TH GRADE
MENDOCINO K-8 ELEMENTARY, MENDOCINO COUNTY
BETH RENSLOW, CLASSROOM TEACHER
HUNTER GAGNON, POET-TEACHER

Friends

We've been friends for seconds, maybe even a minute

I hope this lasts forever, but it's only been an hour

This friendship will keep building for years, even centuries

Now let's go on an adventure until midnight strikes

Then let's hide in a log and feast until dawn

The adventure has only just begun

There is so much more to see all around the universe

Let's travel 'round the world and see what comes up

We'll have the best friendship forever.

ELEANORE SCHIRO, 4TH GRADE
DANA GRAY ELEMENTARY, MENDOCINO COUNTY
JANICE SVERKO, CLASSROOM TEACHER
KAREN LEWIS, POET-TEACHER

Friendship

I am the wind beneath your wings

I dance swiftly in the sky

I sing happy songs of joy

I seek lightning following the thunder

I build onto our friendship like building blocks

We are floating in a whirlpool of friendship

I'm faster than a raging river

In the near future we will still be together

In the dark secrets of heaven

We will always be together, lost in

the maze of friendship.

SARAH MORSE, 4TH GRADE
MENDOCINO K-8 ELEMENTARY, MENDOCINO COUNTY
JOHN MORAN, CLASSROOM TEACHER
KAREN LEWIS AND HUNTER GAGNON, POET-TEACHERS

My Family

My mother told me eat *avocados,*
it's brain food.

My oldest sister told me *read more,*
you'll get better scores.

My second oldest sister told me
talk to her before applying to college
because she's learned the tricks.

My third oldest sister told me
there is lots of homework in middle school,
so enjoy elementary school while you can.

My little sister says *play with me*
because she's bored.

My father says *do your homework*
because I get off topic.

The voices in my head say
do whatever you want to do.

LEWANNA LE, 5TH GRADE
CLEVELAND ELEMENTARY, ALAMEDA COUNTY
MARY LOESER, CLASSROOM TEACHER
MAUREEN HURLEY, POET-TEACHER

Ode to My Sister

Whenever I see a butterfly
I think of my amazing older sister
The one who made me who I am today
The one who gave me a brain, for a memory and thought

Whenever I see a butterfly
I think of my amazing older sister
That starts as a caterpillar,
Becomes a chrysalis,
And into a gorgeous butterfly

Whenever I see a butterfly
I think of my amazing older sister
That is looking down on me during hard and nice times
Flying freely over me

GWEN CHENOWETH, 6TH GRADE
ROOSEVELT ELEMENTARY SCHOOL, SANTA BARBARA
BARBARA BARR, CLASSROOM TEACHER
LALLI DANA DROBNY, POET-TEACHER

My Sister Is Waiting For Me

(after Gwendolyn Brooks)

My sister is waiting for me after school
I walk to her classroom
so we can walk home
Some days she's happy
Some days she's sad
While we walk she talks
on and on about her friends
Somedays they're sweet
Somedays they're sour
Sometimes she's crying
her salty sparkly tears
but I pick her up and tickle her
When I'm not home
she says she misses me
and when I'm sad
she writes me a note saying,
"I em srey."
When I draw something
she tries drawing it, too
She's crazy but funny
annoying but kind
She's mean but
she always says, sorry
Her hair is golden
Her eyes are soft brown
with a spark of crazy
Her small soft hands
grab my own
I smile and hug her
My sister is waiting for me

KAYDEN HAWKS, 5TH GRADE
PARK SCHOOL, MARIN COUNTY
DANNY MARSH, CLASSROOM TEACHER
CLAIRE BLOTTER, POET-TEACHER

My Brother Antonio

My brother Antonio loves to play music,
He plays the piano and the trumpet.
We always used to play together,
but he's thirteen years old and he
gets embarrassed in front of his friends,
but he still loves me.
I'll always remember when he liked
taking pictures when I was three and he was five.
I will always remember when I was about
ten months old how he always gave me
my milk bottle and he gave me a little kiss
on the forehead and said
"I love you."

KAMILA FLORES, 5TH GRADE
MIWOK ELEMENTARY, SONOMA COUNTY
HEIDI DOUGHTY, CLASSROOM TEACHER
SANDRA ANFANG, POET-TEACHER

My Dad

working hard like a spider
making a web
waking early
to wake me making
my breakfast happily
bringing me to soccer

helping me, protecting me
         forgiving me

MAGID REBOUGH, 4TH GRADE
CLAIRE LILIENTHAL SCHOOL, SAN FRANCISCO COUNTY
MS. LEE, CLASSROOM TEACHER
GAIL NEWMAN, POET-TEACHER

Nanny and Papa

Papa is married to Nanny.
Nanny and Papa raised Mom.
Mom raised me, and I wrote this poem.
Papa's breaths are shallow and unpredictable,
His coughing fits are scary and sudden.
I listen every morning for his slow
steps out of the bedroom.
A short cough, a delayed inhale,
the sound of his all too familiar voice offering me
food, food, food.

JOSCELYN BEEBE, 10TH GRADE
WILLITS HIGH SCHOOL, MENDOCINO COUNTY
AMY NORD, CLASSROOM TEACHER
PJ FLOWERS, POET-TEACHER

Great Grandma Marie

If I could go to a Lost and Found, and find someone,
I would find my great grandma, and watch the World Series
with her. She is the reason why my dad and I like the Dodgers.
I would love to see her like my dad did when he was little.
See her without oxygen tubes in her nose, supporting her life.
My dad says that she used to turn on the radio and everyone
would listen. All I want to do is listen to the World Series
with her. I'd hear her tell players that they were "due" for a hit,
and when they got on base, you could hear her say, "Hot Damn!"
I'd give anything to hear her say that one more time. But I can't
just find her at a Lost and Found. For now, we'll hang her jersey
on our fireplace, and hope for the best, knowing somewhere
up there, somebody can be heard, saying, "Hot Damn!"

CARTER LOW, 6TH GRADE
MOUNTAIN VIEW ELEMENTARY, SANTA BARBARA COUNTY
SUSANA YEE, CLASSROOM TEACHER
RON ALEXANDER, POET-TEACHER

Songbird

My mother was a songbird
she used to sing to me
perched
on the foot of my bed
the soul of my childhood
my first memory
a cerulean bird sitting
in a golden cage

My mother was a songbird
she would part her painted lips
lyrics would come
spiraling out
lithe music notes
tiptoeing through the air
melodias ballerinas of sound
lulling me to sleep

The day they came for my father,
My mother was still a songbird
she sang
her sorrows, her tears
her words turned blue
her sadness poured out into music notes
grief wracked her body, her song
shivering
weeping
She sang
and she sang
and she sang

The day they came for my mother,
she was still a songbird
but her cries were no longer harmonious
but desperate pleas
her voice screaming
begging the stern officers
to not take her
send her back to Mexico
away
from me
Tears spilled down her cheeks
my cheeks
I could only stand there
as she begged me to take care of myself
the last note she sang
was a hurried and whispered
"I love you"

My mother was a songbird
Now that she is gone
I can remember the notes that would wash over me
bring a smile to my face,
and I sing
I sing
I sing for her
for every family that is no longer a family
Is a family a family if
there is only one person left?
I sing for the tears that drew tracks down my mother's face.
For the reason that my family was torn apart
for the future families

that will no longer exist
I sing
and I sing
and I sing
so that no family will
ever
have to experience what I have
So that no daughter will have to stand helpless as their mother
is pulled from their embraces
to stand motionless
as their mothers cry and cry and cry
I sing so that change will happen
I sing so that my mother is remembered.
I sing
and I sing
and I sing

JAXI COHEN, 9TH GRADE
LOWELL HIGH SCHOOL, SAN FRANCISCO COUNTY
JENNIFER MOFFITT, CLASSROOM TEACHER
SUSAN TERENCE, POET-TEACHER

Back Through My Life

Go back through those first seconds of your life—
    see your family and love them
Walk and learn for your first time and fall into your mom's grasp—
    you hug her
Find that what you need has always been right there—
    caring and waiting for you
You grow and imagine what life brings you on your journey to heaven
You arrive—it's beautiful just like you imagined—
    peaceful, calm and perfect
You settle down—you think life is amazing—
        and you sleep, dreaming about what happens next

MASON SPESSARD, 4TH GRADE
BROOKS ELEMENTARY SCHOOL, SONOMA
JENNY ANAYA, CLASSROOM TEACHER
JACKIE HUSS HALLERBERG, POET-TEACHER

Remember When

Remember when you had so much
fun shaking with joy.
Remember when you were
scared you were shivering
hoping that it would just end.
Remember when you were
alone and then you felt
like you could never fit in.
Remember when you just
found that friend that could keep
you company.
Remember when you saw the
real world for the first
time.
Remember when you were crying
on your parent's shoulder
and your parent helped you.
Even if you think things are
just left forgotten, please remember
    when.

ISAIAH CASE, 4TH GRADE
MORRIS ELEMENTARY SCHOOL, HUMBOLDT COUNTY
MELIKA HUNEKE, CLASSROOM TEACHER
DAN ZEV LEVINSON, POET-TEACHER

THE FOREST IS WAITING FOR ME

~NATURE POEMS~

The Forest Mother

The forest is waiting for me
I step into its cool green folds
I think up a story in my head
imagining every detail,
line, a movie
birds chirp
sunlight
rustle, crackle
deer
forest eye deer
not green, brown
bounding away
I hear the animals chirping and singing
we love each other
"Kika!" my mom calls
I walk up to my house
"Lunch?" I ask hopefully
"Um, it's almost dinner time!"
Her laughing brown eyes,
she throws me on the bed
I leap back to her,
throwing!
My mother has red-brown hair,
she throws me up, up, up!
I fall back again
the forest
my mother
Kika

KIKA DUNAYEVICH, 5TH GRADE
PARK SCHOOL, MARIN COUNTY
ANDREA DUNN, CLASSROOM TEACHER
CLAIRE BLOTTER, POET-TEACHER

A Cool Summer Day

I was on the field
I felt the wind blow,
the periwinkle and my skin.
It felt like a feather
landing on my shoulder.

HALI WIGHT, 3RD GRADE
MONTECITO UNION SCHOOL, SANTA BARBARA COUNTY
LISA MONSON, CLASSROOM TEACHER
MEGAN YOUNG, POET-TEACHER

Blue White Feather

It reminds me
of the ocean night sky
of magical water

It is the midnight blue river
It is one
of the most beautiful sights

It goes from day to night
in a deep blue ocean
with treasures
of submarines and boats
and a soft singing
with clouds of storms
trees crashing
winds blowing
big waves

people running
just to have
a calm day
small waves

people having fun
calm and happy

It's just
a blue and white feather
sitting on the table

Thank you

for reminding me
of the great blue sea

COLBY THOMSON, 5TH GRADE
PACIFIC UNION SCHOOL, HUMBOLDT COUNTY
CHERYL PAUL, CLASSROOM TEACHER
DARYL NGEE CHINN, POET-TEACHER

The Taste of Plants

The taste of things can last a while,
while others last a day.
Plants can be bitter
salty or sweet
no matter how long they stay
food can be all around us!
no matter what time of day.
The taste of things can last a while,
while others last a day
Plants can be bitter, salty or sweet
no matter how long they stay.
Food is all around us
no matter what time of day
Do you know why plants taste like this?
But as long as the taste stays here,
we will be happy,
because we try new things
every day.

GRACE MONAGHAN, 4TH GRADE
POINSETTIA ELEMENTARY, VENTURA COUNTY
DIANE SATHER AND JULIE SOSKE, CLASSROOM TEACHERS
JENNIFER KELLEY, POET-TEACHER

The Cherry Blossom

The rose red sun
taught me how
to glow in the mirror.

The cherry blossom
taught the spring
how to shine.

The butterfly
sparkling in the sun
teaches the breeze
how to glitter.

How to sing?
(The wind has
secrets to tell you.)

Yuki Wen, 3rd grade
Francis Scott Key Elementary School
San Francisco County
Bonnie Quinn, Classroom Teacher
Susan Terence, Poet-Teacher

On The Hill Over Yonder

The oak remembers
The fresh dew
Resting on his leaves,
glinting like pearls in the
Newborn
morning sun.

He remembers the grins and ringing laughter of
the tiny arms, the tiny legs, as they
Scamper
Up his trunk, hand over hand, foot over toe.

He remembers the deafening
Boom, Crack!
Splitting the sky in two.
And the crying of the clouds,
Chilling him to the bone

He remembers the wind
Yelling
            Screaming
                        Shouting
Whistling in his ear.

He remembers the oranges
Peaches
Reds
Crimsons
Pinks of the sunrise
On yonder horizon
Over hills

Green as jewels

He remembers the cool shade
Of branches
Overhead
Of other, wiser trees,
Now long gone.

He now stands,
Tall as a skyscraper
On the hill over yonder,
He is old and faded
Bark peeling
And alone

But he still remembers.

Amelia Noble, 5th grade
Montecito Union School, Santa Barbara County
Vicky Harbison, Classroom Teacher
Lois Klein, Poet-Teacher

Acorn

Your color is like a horse's coat,
a chestnut color.
You are small in size
but gathering many of you
would make a meal.

Your tip reminds me
of a mechanical pencil
without any lead.

What happened to your cap?
What did it look like?

You are the first food I ate.
You are my nephew's first food.
You remind me that one day
I will have my Ihuk.

Thank you for reminding me
of my family.

Ahtyirahm Allen, 5th grade
Pacific Union School, Humboldt County
Cheryl Paul, Classroom Teacher
Daryl Ngee Chinn, Poet-Teacher

Broken Aspen

Oh, piece of fallen aspen wood,
why were you neglected
and neglected
by the ones you knew the most?
You are merely a small part
of another whole.
Except you are only a part
But what part are you?
The one who feels sadness and regret?
Or perhaps the one who is the most of a threat?
Either way, rain or shine, you were pushed away by friends of thine.
Or were you separated by accident?
Had you been under pressure?
Did you fall because you heard a call of disappointment from
    those above?
Oh sing your song of sadness to me.
Either way, rain or shine, you were pushed away by friends of thine.
Did you leave because of anger?
Did you leave because of shame?
Did you leave because of a little boy who may have insulted
    your name?
Whisper secrets,
thoughts of anger,
and dreams of your mind.
The whole you came from didn't listen,
but I,
I will.

ISABELLA SCHLITT, 5TH GRADE
WEST MARIN SCHOOL, MARIN COUNTY
ESTHER UNDERWOOD, CLASSROOM TEACHER
BRIAN KIRVEN, POET-TEACHER

Morning Glory

The day the flower bloomed,
people just like me were born.
People like me are friends
of nature. We have
a way of life
that only
the stars understand.

I know the songs
of the meteors,
the comets,
the moon.

I have learned
the language
of the planets.

My friends range
from rivers
and streams
to doves
and nightingales.

You see
this is
my way
of life.

Nobody
shall distract me
from this.

ADELE ROBBINS, 3RD GRADE
FRANCIS SCOTT KEY ELEMENTARY SCHOOL,
SAN FRANCISCO COUNTY
SARAH CHAN, CLASSROOM TEACHER
SUSAN TERENCE, POET-TEACHER

Snoglehopher

Above the thunder
there was an earthquake
across the sea
there were waves
beyond the heart
there was love
before the castle
there was a house
after the night
there was day
after the school
there was college

LUKE FOSSE, 5TH GRADE
MENDOCINO K-8 ELEMENTARY, MENDOCINO COUNTY
JOHN MORAN, CLASSROOM TEACHER
HUNTER GAGNON, POET-TEACHER

Anti-Ode to Sand

Oh, sand,
You gritty, scratchy, itchy sand
You scrape my face and skin my knees
Oh, you hide sharp objects
under your cloak of color
I trip and scratch myself
on rocks and sticks and seaweed green
You get in my eyes and make me want to scream.
You get in my mouth and I gag and want to leave
Oh, you stick to the back of my calves and await unseen
Until I get home and realize
I've brought half the beach with me.

ALIA PRENTISS, 6TH GRADE
COASTAL GROVE CHARTER SCHOOL, HUMBOLDT COUNTY
JENNY RUSHBY, CLASSROOM TEACHER
JULIE HOCHFELD, POET-TEACHER

Field of Whispers Heard

A bus, a rumble, a bumble on the move
Filled with waved air and thick breath
A broken seat, meet, feet
Feet meet reflection
Knees can only watch
As her eyes spot that one couple
as her gaze lands on that singular twin
as kids hide from an eye that doesn't see
to do things that she can

A garden of fauna
A field of whispers heard
A nest of birds ready to depart
A green beacon parting noon and what comes after

MAYA LOONEY, 9TH GRADE
SKYLINE HIGH SCHOOL, ALAMEDA COUNTY
AFTERSCHOOL PROGRAM
SOPHIA DAHIN, POET-TEACHER

Point Reyes, California

The beautiful
surf, the waves
pounding on the shore,
the crab, the fish
and whales, beautiful
shimmering bay trees and cows.
Taste mushrooms, "Yum."
The delicious oysters going down
my throat, beautiful hikes,
redwood trees blowing in the wind.
Now I have to go home,
I know, I will sleep good.

KOA WESSNER, 4TH GRADE
WEST MARIN SCHOOL, MARIN COUNTY
ANNE HALLEY-HARPER, CLASSROOM TEACHER
BRIAN KIRVEN, POET-TEACHER

If Point Reyes Was A Person

If Point Reyes was a person
they would be as welcoming as a mother's hug
as diverse as the rocks on her coast
and they would be a little rough around the edges

If Point Reyes was a person
they would always smell like fresh ocean breezes
swirling with morning buns and coffee

If Point Reyes was a person
and a friend was in need they would
wrap them in a blanket of protection and support

If Point Reyes was a person
everyone would know them well,
travel with them on their trails,
explore their beaches
and wade into the waters
that surround our town.

Zoë Rocco-Zilber, 6th grade
West Marin School, Marin County
Peggy Reina, Classroom Teacher
Brian Kirven, Poet-Teacher

Sunrise

As I wake up in bed, I see the sunrise.
Its beautiful yellow light fills the room.
And it's like a floodlight
lighting my sleepy eyes.
I spend the day at school, I go toward home.
On the way home, I see the sunset
like an orange ball going down a hill.
I hear somebody play the piano
so soft and so loud.
Maybe it's just me with the mind of a donkey.
As I reach my porch, the sky is twilight.
I go to bed to experience the same day tomorrow.

KONGTAE KAEWASALAM, 5TH GRADE
CLEVELAND ELEMENTARY, ALAMEDA COUNTY
MARY LOESER, CLASSROOM TEACHER
MAUREEN HURLEY, POET-TEACHER

The Sun Above Me

The sun is a gold flower in the sky.
The sun is like a big diamond
that holds life and light.
The sun is fireworks that never die out.
It's like a diary that holds
my secrets in the sky.
The sun is like the friend
I always had.

Charlotte Perry, 2nd grade
Loma Verde School, Marin County
Gail Petrucelli, Classroom Teacher
Claire Blotter, Poet-Teacher

Cotton from the Clouds

In the wild region of Australia,
a bit of cotton fell from the sky.
It landed upright in the ground
by my tent when I wasn't around.
I picked it up.
What was it?
Was it a pencil?
(Which wasn't yet invented)
Or a magical scepter from ancient ruins?
When I waived it around, clouds formed
in the sky.
And now I am the Master of
Cloud-making.

PALOMA RUDNICKI, 4TH GRADE
MONTECITO UNION SCHOOL, SANTA BARBARA COUNTY
ABBY CARRINGTON, CLASSROOM TEACHER
CIE GUMUCIO, POET-TEACHER

Above the Clouds

When I was a child
above the clouds,
I was with the sun,
blinded from the storm below.
As I descended,
I became earth-bound.
Everything was chaos,
yet no one made a sound.
All were trapped by fear of reality
trying to adjust to humanity.
If only I knew the concept of sanity.

KAIDANCE W., 10TH GRADE
WEST HILLS SCHOOL, MENDOCINO COUNTY
ANNETTE MORRISON, CLASSROOM TEACHER
JABEZ W. CHURCHILL, POET-TEACHER

Moon Musings

I.

moon, oh moon
secrets hidden but still told
with color looks

luna, o luna,
secretos escondidos pero todavia contado
apariencia de color

II.

silver beam, oh
how do you attract the
little bright lights

rayo de plata, o
como atraes las pequeñias
luces brillantes

III.

round reflecting ball,
if no friends, shimmer brightly
to get them

pelota redonda que reflecta,
si no amigos, brilla intensamente
para obtenerios

IV.

big bright moon
your sweet lullabies help everyone
sleep with peace

luna grande y brilliante
tus dulce canciones de cuna ayudah a todos
a dormir con paz

DANIELA LOPEZ ARREGUIN, 4TH GRADE
BROOKS ELEMENTARY SCHOOL, SONOMA COUNTY
JENNY ABBOTT, CLASSROOM TEACHER
JACKIE HALLERBERG, POET-TEACHER

Box

In this box
there is a little crescent moon.
It tries to get out
every single day and moment.
The crescent moon
travels its feelings to me:
fear, nervousness, happiness,
sadness, love, and fun.
This crescent moon always
has peace with itself and always knows
it can't get out. The crescent moon
knows it'll have to wait
'til it's a full moon to have
all of its strength to pull
the lid off of the box.
This moon has always heard silence
and has seen nothing its whole life.
This moon wishes to see the outside
world and everything in it.
This moon wants to see all
the achievements you can get
for being yourself,
and not letting anyone control you.

This crescent moon grows every day,
not knowing
until it's already a full moon.
This moon shines its own light
around itself and looks
at all of the blankness
of the inside of the box.

This moon feels hands touching the sides
Of the box and changes where its original spot was
on the flat surface of a table.
This moon channels peacefulness around it
by closing its eyes and letting it feel
the real power of peace and love.
This little moon wants to touch
the soothing fur of the dog
who is brushing beside the box.

Riley Houston, 5th grade
Pacific Union School, Humboldt County
Cheryl Paul, Classroom Teacher
Daryl Ngee Chinn, Poet-Teacher

How Stars Exist in a Crazy Way

The stars
Stars exist by....

One day ants found five triangles
And they put them in a circle
and made a star and they were throwing it like a ball
One day an ant threw the star so high
that the ant would think it would come back down
but it never came back down
It stayed in the sky
And the ant wanted it back
So they got a lot of triangles and made a lot of stars
but the ant threw all of them in the sky
And the ants threw all of them at night
so the stars only come at night
When the sun came up the ants said,
"Where's the stars?"
But the sun's light is so bright that it covers the stars
and the sky went to black to blue
Then when the moon came up there were the stars
So the ants said,
"So when the sun goes down and the moon comes up,
the stars appear."

They were really surprised.

DANIEL BUSTAMANTE, 4TH GRADE
MIRAMONTE ELEMENTARY SCHOOL, LOS ANGELES COUNTY
TOM LOUIE, CLASSROOM TEACHER
ALICE PERO, POET-TEACHER

Stars

Thank you stars for always shining.
For always being there even if I can't see you.
Thank you.

Even though you are just a fiery ball of gas, you seem gentle.
To me you look how I see you, a piece of sparkling thread
stitched into the quilt that is the night sky.
You look like a diamond, a simple white pinprick of light.
You are like the glare on the sea, bright and beautiful.

You light up the world with your silver glow.
Your best friend, our moon, also shines but you seem to sparkle.
In the sky that is your stage, you are the main attraction.

As the day comes you fade from my view, but you are still there watching.
You come back every night as if to say "I am here, I will stay."
Your shape is shown as a five sided shape of points, it represents you well.
The points show that you are beautiful, yes, but strong.

Some say you make pictures, but I only see the beauty
of what you are, not what you can be.
You are like pearls dropping into the deep blue of the ocean.
You scatter along my paper, making it have beauty as well.

You will always be glowing, shining, beautiful you.

Keep shining stars.

Lea Anderson, 6th grade
Roosevelt Elementary School, Santa Barbara
Barbara Barr, Classroom Teacher
Lalli Dana Drobny, Poet-Teacher

What the Night Hears

What can the night hear?
Can it hear the beeping of cars
as the people drive home?
Can it hear the click of lights going out
as people go to sleep?
Can it hear the flip-flip of book's pages
as someone reads "Good Night"?
Can it hear the thump-thump
of the nocturnal animals' hearts as they hunt for food?
Can it hear the splash of the ocean
as it hits the dark shadowy rocks?
Can it hear the shhhh of people
breathing in their sleep?
Can it hear the tick-tick-tick of the clock
ticking to sunrise?
Can it hear the soft pit-pat
as the rays of sun hit the window?
Can it hear the sun and moon swooshing over
to the other side of the world and back?

MADISON MEREDITH, 3RD GRADE
TAM VALLEY ELEMENTARY, MARIN COUNTRY
KAREN O'TOOLE, CLASSROOM TEACHER
PRARTHO SERENO, POET-TEACHER

Nature's Music

Reeds, when the wind blows I hear the soft
song of nature's flute
Ice like diamonds of cold winter or
the wondrous tranquility of Aurora Borealis
The willow's weeping branches like the
untuned strings of a harp
Sapphire, like the small parts of blue
sky, through the tight branches of the
leafless icy tree in winter
Snakes, like the dragons of old leaping
through the sky of earth's soft dirt
The snow, as if the shimmers of the rainbow
trapped in a small box
Silver, like the slick scales of a fish or
a shining ball of light
The moon, the sun's brother, cloaked in the
blanket of the night's sky

Cole Jayme, 4th grade
Loma Verde School, Marin County
Karen McCormish, Classroom Teacher
Claire Blotter, Poet-Teacher

Silvery Golden Sounds

I love the keys of the piano blowing into my ears
from a long distance, but still so so loud
it never fades away—even when no one is playing it.

I love the tweet of the birds singing
in the early bright morning, and the splash of water
against the ocean rocks while I'm walking across the beach.

And I love the dolphins and whales
breaching out of the water and diving out
again and again: splash, splash!

I love the wind blowing in my ears,
and the screech of the mice scampering
across the floor to find cheese for their baby mice.

I love the rattly dance of the tall tall tallest trees
blowing in the wind. And I love the flowers
in spring sprouting and turning into buds.
And the bud turning into a flower
that is hanging on a tree in the blowy wind.

And I love the sound of the fairies opening their flower doors
and closing them again and again.

ALLIE ANDRESEN, 1ST GRADE
STRAWBERRY POINT ELEMENTARY, MARIN COUNTY
KIMBERLY RUSSEL, CLASSROOM TEACHER
PRARTHO SERENO, POET-TEACHER

The Sky

The sky is an endless roof
It swallows the clouds in its loving arms
It is never ending blue and black
The sky is held up by the mountains

It swallows the clouds in its loving arms
The sky is silent like the wind
The sky is held up by the mountains
The sky is like the ocean pulling things in it

The sky is silent like the wind
The sky is like a shield protecting us from space
The sky is like the ocean pulling things in
The sky hasn't begun or ended its silent race

The sky is like a shield protecting us from space
It is never ending blue and black
The sky hasn't begun or ended its silent race
The sky is an endless roof.

AUSTIN PRESLEY, 5TH GRADE
APPLE BLOSSOM SCHOOL, SONOMA COUNTY
DYLAN LICCIARDO, CLASSROOM TEACHER
LISA SHULMAN, POET-TEACHER

Give Me A Planet Like Pluto

With a planet like that,
I could see all the stars
from the other side of the galaxy
shimmering pitch blackness of space.
I could hear the silence
being the only surviving soul
for light years.
I could hide myself from terrors and voices
from the distant world of humanity.
I could travel on icy lands and slopes
with such swiftness and ease.
I could feel the icy air travel tirelessly.
I could find life from another species
of amazing and wonderful creatures.

When it's time to fly,
give me a planet like that!

RYAN WU, 6TH GRADE
HAMILTON SCHOOL, MARIN COUNTY
JON ANGER, CLASSROOM TEACHER
TERRI GLASS, POET-TEACHER

The Living Planet

The one that is blue
It has tears in its eyes
It's crying inside
It sounds like it's crying upon us
In the shadows of space
It looks like it's coming out
Shyness up alone
In space.

SUMMER HURST, 2ND GRADE
REDWOOD ELEMENTARY, MENDOCINO COUNTY
MONICA LIMA, CLASSROOM TEACHER
KAREN LEWIS AND HUNTER GAGNON, POET-TEACHERS

How to Be Fire

Rip away branches
as you eat at a tree

Smash everything in your way

Make the sky dark and gray
with smoke

Shrivel every blossom til
there is nothing left
but your flames

TRUETT SHEEHY, 2ND GRADE
MONTECITO UNION SCHOOL, SANTA BARBARA COUNTY
HEIDI CRAINE, CLASSROOM TEACHER
LOIS KLEIN, POET-TEACHER

Fire

I have the grace and beauty of a sunset over the ocean
I also am as dangerous as the mighty tigers
People fear me and act like the world is ending
The firefighters put me out of my raging stage
and I become as gentle as a kitten.
I burn forests to get my revenge on the people
Treating me as if I were just another item
So, for my revenge I take their items.
I am also useful because when my anger is out
The saplings I left behind bring back life.

Catherine Petty, 6th grade
Tomales Elementary, Marin County
Jennifer Warner, Classroom Teacher
Brian Kirven, Poet-Teacher

Water

Thank you water
as you cool me down on a
hot summer day

Thank you water
for I use you in my tea

Thank you water
for you are used
in many things

Thank you water
as I use you to water
my plants

Thank you water
as you fall to the ground
when it rains

Thank you water
as you stream down
the waterfall

Thank you water
for without you
we would not
have life

CADENCE LU, 3RD GRADE
COLD SPRING SCHOOL, SANTA BARBARA COUNTY
BECKI GONZALEZ, CLASSROOM TEACHER
MEGAN YOUNG, POET-TEACHER

The Spirit of Water
(inspired by Freedom Wings)

blue dances
in golden sunrise
a person
with outstretched arms
is frozen inside—
feels cold but so alive

Stela Clark, 3rd grade
Richard Bard Elementary, Ventura County
Katya Acuna, Classroom Teacher
Fernando Salinas, Poet-Teacher

It's Raining Very Hard

It's raining nickels and pickles

It's raining chicks and bricks

It's raining seagulls and beagles

It's raining fire and tires

It's raining tomatoes and potatoes

It's raining vans and cans

It's raining boxes and foxes

It's raining chairs and bears

It's raining on me and my friends

EMILY SILVA, 3RD GRADE
DANA GRAY ELEMENTARY, MENDOCINO COUNTY
ERIN SMITH, CLASSROOM TEACHER
KAREN LEWIS, POET-TEACHER

Rain is Falling

Rain is falling on my nose
It's falling on my toes
I wish I was rain
for rain has no pain
Sometimes I wonder, I wonder...
If rain had no pain...
Would it be crying?

And if it was crying,
Would people always be sad?
And if people were always sad
Would there be any rainbows?
And if there were no rainbows,
where would my joy come from?
And I think if the sea was black
would I swim in it?

But I say no!
I will always be happy
no matter what the weather,
my happiness will shine
and I will never fall into
the dark hole of "what ifs?"

I will always glow.

AMAYA TROCKEL, 5TH GRADE
TOMALES ELEMENTARY, MARIN COUNTY
MEREDITH LEASK, CLASSROOM TEACHER
BRIAN KIRVEN, POET-TEACHER

Rain

The rain is a doctor, healing living
things wherever it ventures,
plummeting down over the cliffs,
the houses, and the people below.
On some days, the rain is
wearing a fat gray cloud, while
on the others, it is smiling a
gentle drizzle.

CLODAGH MCINTYRE, 4TH GRADE
CLAIRE LILIENTHAL SCHOOL, SAN FRANCISCO COUNTY
MS. CARRILLO, CLASSROOM TEACHER
GAIL NEWMAN, POET-TEACHER

AND IF THERE WERE
NO RAINBOWS

My Heart

My heart is the desolate desert valley I was born in;
the endless
landscape full of sagebrush
blue birds humming songs
like my pulse
my home that's nestled between mountains
Nana's rum cake and cobalt eyes that do nothing to hide her fire.
Pookie's smiles as sweet as buttercream, and his hearty laugh.
Casinos that fill your lungs with smoke, and your head with good times.
Daddy Dear, whose mind never lost its sharpness,
even as the life left his bones.
Lights from the strip lighting up even the darkest parts of the valley.
Summers that lasted longer
than most lives, and
winters over in the blink of an eye.
Games of wallball and tag until the street lights went out.
Sunsets so beautiful, you could cry.
The place that wasn't all that good, in fact wasn't good at
all, but was my home.

MARLEENA LIMBRICK, 7TH GRADE
WALTER REED MIDDLE SCHOOL, LOS ANGELES COUNTY
DANIELLE DAGILIS, CLASSROOM TEACHER
JESSICA M. WILSON, POET-TEACHER

Her Mind

Her
mind is like a whirlpool
Dive
too deep you'll meet the girl whose
Soft
side turns to dust
The
beginning, we've only discussed
Go
deeper, if you must
You'll
find yourself a hurricane
Only
then you'll see her pain
Venture
farther, just gets darker
Finally
it stops
Then
it starts to twist and twirl
You're
no longer in that girl...

Delilah Tarr, 5th grade
Strawberry Point School, Marin County
Rachel Quek, Classroom Teacher
Terri Glass, Poet-Teacher

Shy

Sad flies away
away sad flies
two o two
I won't run
don't hide
the sadness is part of me
no matter how hard I try
so go, go so
what, don't leave me, no
no me leave don't
it is something a part
part a something is it
hello wait
wait hello there's something
no one else knows
come back.

AUBREY PINE, 4TH GRADE
PRESTWOOD ELEMENTARY, SONOMA COUNTY
SHANNON MCCAMBRIDGE, CLASSROOM TEACHER
SANDRA ANFANG, POET-TEACHER

Shyness

Shyness is a pink sky at the middle of dawn,

a flute playing when you're getting pelted by hail.

Shyness is a tulip sitting in the middle of the forest,

a planet holding nothing but stars.

It is a minnow swimming at a reef with nothing to eat,

a winter with no snow.

Shyness is silence over and over,

the line between sad and peace.

Shyness is the person with no one to play with,

an airplane with no people.

Max Pasquale, 3rd grade
Loma Verde School, Marin County
Ali McMorrow, Classroom Teacher
Claire Blotter, Poet-Teacher

Envy

My feelings mock
Me like the birds
In the trees
I see them chirping
As happy as could be.
As I admire them,
Envy grows inside me.
Why must I be envious?
I thought I was free.

ARIEL REYES, 11TH GRADE
WILLITS HIGH SCHOOL, MENDOCINO COUNTY
AMY NORD, CLASSROOM TEACHER
PJ FLOWERS, POET-TEACHER

Sad Life

I am as stiff as a
rock. Have you ever
seen a person you
   love die? Nothing
   fills the air. My sad
   life. I am sad.
   My grandfather has
   passed. Nothing still
   fills the air. I am still
   sad. My sad life.
   A year has
   passed and I am
   still sad. Life is
   sad. Rain fills
   the air.

Nya Flynn, 3rd grade
Morris Elementary School, Humboldt County
Nanci Zanone, Classroom Teacher
Dan Zev Levinson, Poet-Teacher

Fear is Like a Window

Fear is like a window
sometimes you can escape
sometimes you cannot.
You can stare at it but not do anything.
Try to jump out but nothing happens.
It feels like you are trapped in a room.

ELLA ROSE VON JUNSCH, 3RD GRADE
APPLE BLOSSOM SCHOOL, SONOMA COUNTY
LISA SHULMAN, CLASSROOM TEACHER
LISA SHULMAN, POET-TEACHER

Fear Is a Teenage Boy

Fear is a
teenage boy
with shredded up clothes
and a hood over his head
pranking the weak
but he just wants
to make a friend.

Vinnie Hamann, 3rd grade
Apple Blossom School, Sonoma County
Robin Lintz, Classroom Teacher
Lisa Shulman, Poet-Teacher

Loneliness

loneliness
a cold icy
  breeze that
    falls through the
      pitch black streets
      trickles down
    the stairs of the
      old apartment
        building it shoots
      through the air
      like icy cement
      a wind of
        fear a black
        darkness
          on the
          deserted
          streets,
      a black wind
        a bullet streaking
          the sky,
          loneliness.

HAVEN ARMISTEAD, 5TH GRADE
PARK SCHOOL, MARIN COUNTY
ANDREA DUNN, CLASSROOM TEACHER
CLAIRE BLOTTER, POET-TEACHER

Loneliness is Like a World with No People

Loneliness is like a world with
no people, it's like being blind,
with no one to hear you, call for
help, loneliness is like a baby
with no family, loneliness is like
a soccer ball in a field, with
no one to kick it,
loneliness is like the last puppy
for adoption that never got
adopted, loneliness is like
a world with no sun,
loneliness is like
a lost friendship,
loneliness is like a dead flower,
loneliness is as painful
as 100 tubes through your
body, loneliness is like
a happy little frog, but all
of a sudden, its lungs stop
working,
                    B*A*M ! just
        like * that, loneli *ness is
like being in a giant, blank,
empty room, with nowhere to
go, loneliness . . . loneliness . . . loneliness . . . .

BRISTAHL ADAMS, 6TH GRADE
GARFIELD ELEMENTARY SCHOOL, HUMBOLDT COUNTY
ALAINA KELLEY, CLASSROOM TEACHER
DAN ZEV LEVINSON, POET-TEACHER

Pain

Pain will come,
let it visit,
cry it out.
Bleed it out.
Then ask it to leave.
Do not allow it to build a home
and call it broken.
We aren't meant
to be broken forever,
that is punishment
to our heart
and mind.

VIOLET CASTILLO-OSMAN, 6TH GRADE
TOMALES ELEMENTARY, MARIN COUNTY
JENNIFER WARNER, CLASSROOM TEACHER
BRIAN KIRVEN, POET-TEACHER

When I Am...

When I am mad
it feels like a bunch of pieces of glass
in my stomach

When I am sad
it feels like I lost my best friend

When I am bored
it feels like I am a rusty old house

ALEXIE GUTIERREZ, 3RD GRADE
DELPHI ACADEMY, LOS ANGELES COUNTY
GRANT YOUN, CLASSROOM TEACHER
ALICE PERO, POET-TEACHER

Dark Walks Alone

Every Night the tall, skinny
Boy walked the dark cold streets
Alone. Every night the tall skinny boy
Walked longer than the last night before
Every night the tall skinny boy had
Insomnia worse than the night before, so
Every night the tall skinny boy walked
More and more until
The tall skinny boy was lost forever.
The people of the town quickly forgot
The tall skinny boy who would
Walk and walk and walk.

JOEY JIMENEZ, 12TH GRADE
SAN ANDREAS HIGH SCHOOL, SAN BENITO COUNTY
JEANENE SEILER, CLASSROOM TEACHER
AMANDA CHIADO, POET-TEACHER

That Was Then

Hot breath in a cold room.
Blankets on the floor,
Children running and parents yelling,
But that was then.
Hot chicken soup on a sick day,
Gravelly sand in running shoes,
Little bugs on his hands,
Yet, that was then.
Memories passing with every second,
Noses pressed against flowers,
And colors seen against other colors.
The smell of other people in a room,
That was then.
Birds singing on emerald trees,
A family on a picnic,
The sound of kids laughing,
But that was then.
A small room with many people,
People with people with mutual feelings,
Paint on paper and faces,
The dripping of water on concrete,
Yet, that was then.
Everything was then,
Everything is now.
But, that was then.

ANONYMOUS, 10TH GRADE
WILLITS HIGH SCHOOL, MENDOCINO COUNTY
AMY NORD, CLASSROOM TEACHER
PJ FLOWERS, POET-TEACHER

Enough

"too fat" she is to you
"too skinny" she becomes
nothing that she does will ever be enough
she does everything to please you she skips a meal,
tries to lose a few
her teeth are crooked
her hair's a mess
they tell her to change the style,
"go put on a dress."
the alarm rings at 5 for her to wake up
time for her to put on her makeup.
she's got the clear skin and the pretty smile,
but even then they make her go the extra mile
she has to have the newest iphone
she's not wearing the newest clothes so she cries on the ride home
how can we feel okay when the standards are too rough
the supermodels on magazines are already "perfect" enough,
but society says even they have a flaw;
she's too flat
put on a bigger bra.
she wants to satisfy you,
but when she does she is "trying too hard"
she wants to be herself, but she has to play the part.
no one is perfect
and no one ever will be
everyone needs their own form of beauty.
society will never be satisfied,
so believe you are beautiful while being happy inside.

SKYE TORRES, 7TH GRADE
WALTER REED MIDDLE SCHOOL, LOS ANGELES COUNTY
DANIELLE DAGILIS, CLASSROOM TEACHER
JESSICA M. WILSON, POET-TEACHER

Blood Stone

Clear space.
Clear nothingness.
A sea of cloudless dreams
lost wishes, lost hopes
snatched away from Life's hands
by death.
A clouded sky
and then
a supernova
filled in anger with tears.
Drops of blood
trapped inside a smooth surface.
The crimson light,
in the eyes of Life
As he releases what once was
A blood stone.

Nora Ross, 5th grade
Old Mill School, Marin County
Sarah Funk, Classroom Teacher
Terri Glass, Poet-Teacher

Death's Door

It happens
Every time you go outside, you can die.
Every time you eat, you can choke.
Every time you sleep, you could never wake up.
Every time you swim, you could drown.
Every time you run, you could fall.
Every time you cross the street, you could get hit.
Every time you get sick, you could die.
These are risks we have to take,
to live life.
With death comes sadness.
With sadness comes misery.
With misery comes depression.
With depression comes
lethal self harm.

EVERETT GALLAGHER, 6TH GRADE
WEST MARIN SCHOOL, MARIN COUNTY
PEGGY REINA, CLASSROOM TEACHER
BRIAN KIRVEN, POET-TEACHER

Remember

I remember silver
grey hair, bright blue
eyes and a wide smile

I remember my
grandpa lying in
bed with my
grandma until his
heart stopped, a rhythm
stopped and it was
completely silent

I remember

NANAMI FULLER, 4TH GRADE
COLD SPRING ELEMENTARY, SANTA BARBARA COUNTY
KELLY ORWIG, CLASSROOM TEACHER
RON ALEXANDER, POET-TEACHER

Worries, Worries All Comin' Up

Worry is like mountains
falling on top of you

Worry is like homeless
puppies

Worry is like
falling water

Worry is like
hard rain drops

Worry is like people
bullying you

Worry is like getting
watched

Worry is like dragons
attacking you

Worry is like
losing your dog

Worry is like people
you know dying

EMILY WALSH, 3RD GRADE
LOMA VERDE SCHOOL, MARIN COUNTY
LESLIE ROBERTSON AND JESSICA CRUZ, CLASSROOM TEACHERS
CLAIRE BLOTTER, POET-TEACHER

Lunacy

Is that a bloodstain?
No, that's a mark of my growing womanhood

The moon has abandoned me
Instead pulling the tides between my loins

It is not blood
It is an animalistic ritual

The moon pouring through my window
On my fifteenth birthday

It is not blood
But the tears of my father

The moon highlights the streams down his cheeks
He never wanted this day to come

It is not blood
It is the afterbirth of my new life

The moon sharpens the steel in my mother's eyes
Soon she will teach me how to survive

It is not blood
It is too dark to come from my heart

The moon grins maniacally at my desires
Too deep and strange to understand

Is that a bloodstain?

No, it is the end of an era of innocence

The moon has abandoned me
The warm hues of dawn open their arms

Genesis Perez, 12th grade
Channel Islands High School, Ventura County
Nicholas Schlesinger, Classroom Teacher
Fernando Salinas, Poet-Teacher

La Verguenza

Quiero decir algo pero la verguenza me impide.
A veces yo…!! Le temo o me impide decir
las cosas. It's a battle sin fin y me pregunto
que haré en este momento!! Y yo en este momento
quisiera desaparecer. "One day," I said,
"En esta guerra, I will be the winner. Forever."
Este momento ha llegado. Muchos días pasaron
hasta que al fin gané. Ni yo supe, pero un día perdí
the shame in the class. Me sentí muy bien. It is
unos of the best days in my life. Y me siento muy orgulloso.

The Shame

I want to say something, but my shame stops me.
Sometimes I…!! fear to say something.
It's an endless battle, and I ask myself
"What should I do in this moment?" In this moment
I want to disappear. "One day," I said,
"In this war, I will be the winner, forever."
That day has come. A lot of days passed,
but I won. I don't know how, but I lost my shame.
It feels great, I feel great. It is
one of the best days in my life. And I feel really proud of myself!!

Brandon Tamayo, 6th grade
James Monroe Elementary School, Sonoma County
Nikki Winovich, Classroom Teacher
Phyllis Meshulam, Poet-Teacher

Spirit

I see a man everyday but not any man, a homeless man
Just because he is on the streets no money, no food,
no proper home and no food he still holds something.
Something special. Something most wealthy men do
not have. He has a spirit, he strums that guitar
and tunes his life with his music.
You must go through pain but also endure pain.
He holds the spirit in his hands and knows
no one will ever be able to take that away from him.

PHILIPPA McKEVITT, 6TH GRADE
NEW ROADS SCHOOL, LOS ANGELES COUNTY
ALEX RAND, CLASSROOM TEACHER
INDIA RADFAR, POET-TEACHER

Have You Ever Left Someone?

I have—
    it's hard
your heart hurts
    you feel lost
the person
    is everything
to you
    it's like you're
in a dark room
    without anyone
then, you see them
    just want to hug them
when you cry
    your tears are like
their memories
    you remember the moments
you had with them
    & it feels like
they are
    with you

Alaa Al-Badani, 6th grade
Anna Yates Elementary, Alameda County
Ashante Smith, Classroom Teacher
Brennan DeFrisco, Poet-Teacher

Imagina

Imagina a las personas que sueñan,
la gente que quiere una oportunidad
pero renunciar a la esperanza cuando aparecen
nadie los acepta, lloran en
vergüenza en el fondo, todo lo que queda detrás
para empezar de nuevo como una nueva persona
o lo hacen quédate lo mismo—
imagina

Imagine

Imagine the people who dream,
the people who want an opportunity
but give up hope when it appears
no one accepts them, they cry in
shame deep inside, everything left behind
to start over like a new person
or do they stay the same—
just imagine

CESAR JARQUIN FLORES, 5TH GRADE
OAK GROVE ELEMENTARY, SONOMA COUNTY
DEBRA LEONARD, CLASSROOM TEACHER
BRENNAN DEFRISCO, POET-TEACHER

Placement

Is placement necessary—

Shouldn't we all get along
not pushed into a place
and categorized
as one of that place
for life, punished
by drama when you try
to move from place to place

Then asked why
you didn't stay
in one place

Yet, the questioner
wouldn't be willing
to step out of place
to come to you

Am I the only one
put in place / am I
that one chess piece
that moves less than the others

If not are we all in the same position,
is there no queen or king
and we are all just the board,
not the pieces?

CAITLIN O'DONNELL, 5TH GRADE
OAK GROVE ELEMENTARY, SONOMA COUNTY
DEBRA LEONARD, CLASSROOM TEACHER
BRENNAN DEFRISCO, POET-TEACHER

Lost Time

Disappearing
Days, weeks, months go by
Like a tree losing its leaves
It goes too fast
Where does all this lost time go?
I don't know
Do you?
Where does all this lost time go
Flying away like those lost leaves
Flying away, so close you can almost touch it
But you know it's gone
It flies away, faster than it should
Disappears quickly
Too quickly
All that lost time
Flying away

JADYN FENYVES-WARD, 5TH GRADE
CLEVELAND ELEMENTARY, ALAMEDA COUNTY
MARY LOESER, CLASSROOM TEACHER
MAUREEN HURLEY, POET-TEACHER

Drama

I sit
in the corner crying. I hear my
friends scream.
I cry when my friends scream.

I sit
in the corner arguing with the voices
in my head. I hear my friends cry.
I scream in my head when I hear my friends cry.

I sit
in the corner screaming. I hear
my friends fight. I scream
when I hear my friends fight.

I sit
in the corner blocking out
the drama. I hear the
drama attacking my friends.
I hate drama.

Calypso Olstad, 4th grade
Dana Gray Elementary, Mendocino County
Lynette May, Classroom Teacher
Karen Lewis, Poet-Teacher

Culture

Imagine it's your first day of high school
and you know no one and someone
walks up to you and says, "Are you Chinese?"
And you answer him with the little voice you have.
With that, he says out loud with a thundering voice,
"Hey, everyone that has a cat and dog, keep them
away from him. He'll eat them."
Then you're about to speak up
but your voice doesn't come up
because your body rejects your voice
at that time in your mind.
You say he shouldn't say that
when he knows nothing about your culture.

KAI GAO, 6TH GRADE
JAMES MONROE ELEMENTARY, SONOMA COUNTY
MIKE PERSINGER, CLASSROOM TEACHER
PHYLLIS MESHULAM, POET-TEACHER

Where You From?

I'm from a good place
turned bad,
taste of jail bread in my mouth.
The road I walk,
a dead end,
a place of sadness and destruction.
I'm from where the system
closes its fingers around me.

GIO L., 9TH GRADE
WEST HILLS SCHOOL, MENDOCINO COUNTY
ANNETTE MORRISON, CLASSROOM TEACHER
JABEZ W. CHURCHILL, POET-TEACHER

Pocho

I was born and raised
pocho
in Fort Bragg,
small town,
on the outskirts of the bay.
Million dollar homes
with views of Noyo Harbor
I will never own.
Schools,
escuelas mexicanas en mi querido rancho,
I will never attend.
Tambien soy panza verde,
green-belly,
cactus fed,
de Leon Guanajuato,
Isla de las Momias.

CARLOS G., 11TH GRADE
WEST HILLS SCHOOL, MENDOCINO COUNTY
ANNETTE MORRISON, CLASSROOM TEACHER
JABEZ W. CHURCHILL, POET-TEACHER

Pony Tail

Pony tail
warrior's prayer
comes from within.

KODY I., 12TH GRADE
WEST HILLS SCHOOL, MENDOCINO COUNTY
DIANA BLUNDELL, CLASSROOM TEACHER
JABEZ W. CHURCHILL, POET-TEACHER

No Es La Luna

No es la luna
lo que veo
de mi celda

No Moon

It's not the moon
I see
looking from my cell

LUIS A., 9TH GRADE
WEST HILLS SCHOOL, MENDOCINO COUNTY
DIANA BLUNDELL, CLASSROOM TEACHER
JABEZ W. CHURCHILL, POET-TEACHER

Time

They say
I'm a bad person,
a menace.
Put me in a box
away from society,
family and friends,
the streets,
good times.
I'm in a box thinking,
reminiscing,
about time.

DIEGO V., 10TH GRADE
WEST HILLS SCHOOL, MENDOCINO COUNTY
DIANA BLUNDELL, CLASSROOM TEACHER
JABEZ W. CHURCHILL, POET-TEACHER

Safe Place

I don't have a safe place,
nowhere to call home.
I miss those days,
my house.
It feels so long ago I had a place called home.
Now, I wander through these streets.
It smells of oil and grease.
In these musty streets I roam,
I see dealers and junkies.
Most, without a home.
Drugs and drinks all around.
Just want another dose.
Can't seem to get away.
Feel so trapped and all alone.
A struggle every day.

CODY M., 10TH GRADE
WEST HILLS SCHOOL, MENDOCINO COUNTY
DIANA BLUNDELL, CLASSROOM TEACHER
JABEZ W. CHURCHILL, POET-TEACHER

On Meditation

Eyes open,
eyes closed,
all the same.
A storm,
lightning all around.
Monsters attacking,
not safe and sound.
People screaming,
people fighting.
Dogs bark.
The clouds get cloudier.
The rain starts pouring.
Everything gets silent.
And the clock
stops ticking.

Aleah F., 10th grade
West Hills School, Mendocino County
Diana Blundell, Classroom Teacher
Jabez W. Churchill, Poet-Teacher

Locked Up

Locked up
behind bars.
Should've never gotten in that car.
The system tears families apart.
Locked up,
told when and what to do.
The people who stick with you,
very few.
Sleeping on concrete,
I miss my bed.
Kids end up in prison
or end up dead.
Wish I would have listened
to what my mom said.

GIOVANNI L., 10TH GRADE
WEST HILLS SCHOOL, MENDOCINO COUNTY
DIANA BLUNDELL, CLASSROOM TEACHER
JABEZ W. CHURCHILL, POET-TEACHER

I Would Fly Away

I'm afraid of losing my mind
because when I do
there ain't gonna be another night,
another lonely night.
I hate myself,
I really do.
If someone,
somebody really felt my pain,
they wouldn't be able to get through.
I remember I had a place called home.
But now, everywhere I go,
don't feel like home.
In this lonely cage
where everybody says they feel your pain,
if I could,
I would fly away.
But there's no place to go.
If there was,
I would fly away.

Bryan G. , 10th grade
West Hills School, Mendocino County
Diana Blundell, Classroom Teacher
Jabez W. Churchill, Poet-Teacher

Facil/Easy

¿De donde eres?
Where you from?
Where dope-fiends look to score
another hit, another high.
Homicide, another homicide,
driving families insane.
En mi barrio, my hood,
you can taste the blood,
the slugs, the pain.
?De donde eres?
Where you from?
Another barrio *donde es facil*
where it's easy to get money
selling drugs or hitting robberies
¿De donde eres?
Where you from?
Un barrio donde la gente me critica por delinquente,
judge me as delinquent,
por mi raza
y mis tatuajes en la cara
for my race and the tattoos on my face.
¿De donde eres?

BRYAN S., 11TH GRADE
WEST HILLS SCHOOL, MENDOCINO COUNTY
DIANA BLUNDELL, CLASSROOM TEACHER
JABEZ W. CHURCHILL, POET-TEACHER

Unique

Why is it every day and night, every sun and moon,
some mistreat our blood?
Tons of us all around the world have accents.
From Mexico to Ireland to just about anywhere.
We've lived in these places, we've lived in these homes;
and when it's already hard to leave,
others say things like, "What did you say?",
with some type of grin that throws you off after you speak.

It's not like people can change their voices, their blood;
these voices are what they have, what we have.

I've grown up in America with all accents and languages,
and as I travel through Europe, I hear
accents and languages and think they're so unique,
and I don't have one.

My mom is British and has an accent.
I don't recognize it, but I know it's there.
You know what else I hear?
I hear people making fun of them;
acting all rude because their voice is different,
their voice is unique!

We don't get to decide where we're from or where we're born.
When you come to seek a new country, you see future; not hate.

To think that in this world there is that hatred and not just

acceptance where you don't feel
welcome, is terrible.

We all have amazing voices because we are unique.

ELLA HOBSON, 7TH GRADE
WALTER REED MIDDLE SCHOOL, LOS ANGELES COUNTY
DANIELLE DAGILIS, CLASSROOM TEACHER
JESSICA M. WILSON, POET-TEACHER

Our Country

I watch America win, I watch America lose.
I watch our country's flag wave in the sunlight.
I watch America in pain, and I watch America laugh.
I watch America fight with its head held high.
America is not always fair, it is not always right.
America has judged people by their skin color.
America has been mean,
America has been proud.
America is trying to change and so should you.
I watch the sunset, I watch the sun rise,
but I have never seen any as beautiful as in America.

NATALIE BANTON, 5TH GRADE
LOMA VERDE SCHOOL, MARIN COUNTY
LISA HANLEY, CLASSROOM TEACHER
CLAIRE BLOTTER, POET-TEACHER

The Cage We Made

I find it hard to accept the world right now
With confusion and trickery and fools like *wow*.
How can you be so dumb?
A planet filled with babies sucking their thumbs.

I mean right here right now
We could be cleaning our towns
Fixing our streets and healing our wounds
Helping the planet instead of dying too soon.

But instead we hide, abide and bow
And follow the pasture rout, like a cow
Controlled by our ignorance, to stay content
But we all feel the regret in the end.

We hide from pain only to feel the spice and burn
Of others who decided to take control of your turn,
We smell the ash of wood and trash
But we miss the fact that it's life that has crashed.

You dredge beyond the here and now
Only to find yourself stuck in the crowd
And you beg and beg for time to start
But you made the choice to end your mark.

And with that said, you come to see
The futile, endless inevitability
Of the world we made to cover fear
That keeps us stuck in the now and here.

AMON B. CHAVEZ, 12TH GRADE
EAST HIGH SCHOOL, HUMBOLDT COUNTY
JEN FEMENELLA, CLASSROOM TEACHER
DAN ZEV LEVINSON, POET-TEACHER

the long ride

reflecting
reflecting on the friends i've made
reflecting on the friends i've lost
the people i've loved
he never did
i feel like my life is a race car track
and i am the car
except there is no finish line or end
just repeating
going around
around
around
and around again
turn after turn after turn after turn
and i am constantly living the same hell
day by day by day by day
i hear them you know
the voices on the bus
on the street
in the stores
people acting so sweet
yet really so cruel
fake smiles passing
through the endless aisles
in the local grocery store
middle fingers raising from the
half- down tinted windows of the
family car
the young ones insulting each other
like it is okay
the bullying

the body shaming
the put downs
the homophobic slurs
the dirty looks
it's like a trend now-a-days
recording fights for the views
posting bullying for the likes
and it's like society is on the track
the neverending
the endless
the long ride
—and it won't change unless we do something about it

EMMA CROWE, 10TH GRADE
WILLITS HIGH SCHOOL, MENDOCINO COUNTY
AIMEE NORD, CLASSROOM TEACHER
PJ FLOWERS, POET-TEACHER

The Questions

If you have a technology device,
you have access to more info than any
human in history
but you probably don't care.
That curiosity we once had about the world is gone.

Why is it the older we get, the less questions we ask?
Throughout history, we have always accepted the world we were
born into
and if anyone tried to question our world,
they were looked down upon.

It's only years later, we look back and ask ourselves –
how could anyone accept that world?
Today we call ourselves developed
as if we have nothing left to learn
but within one hundred years, people will
look back and they, too, will ask that
question.

It's no secret that our world is full
of problems.
We rally.
We protest.
Still the problems only seem to grow.
Maybe, because they stem from a much
larger
problem
we fail
to see.

DeAngelo Martinez, 5th grade
Brooks Elementary School, Sonoma County
Patti Dearth, Classroom Teacher
Jackie Huss Hallerberg, Poet-Teacher

213

LA Poem

Out of 712,919 people in the 33rd district, I got to meet my friends
My teachers and I got to be with my family.
My education is one of the 169,955 people.
My home is one of 154,133 that are rented.
That is my LA.
The LA where people don't care
The LA where people are swag
The LA where people throw away fate
The LA where I am
The LA where a beach is made
The LA where eating is good
The LA where safety is a lie
The LA where no life is guaranteed
The LA where flights soar up into the sky
The LA where the tornado of trash is visible everywhere
My LA
Your LA
Our LA
The LA
The waves
The sand
The rocks
The chains made of gold
The begging not finding luck
The thriller rides
The lines
The crowds
The movies
The water parks
Universal studios
The place where the protest is popular.

The place where protest might be popular but beliefs are strong.
The place where nothing will be believed by everyone
The place where answers cannot be guaranteed
Where you can find nothing but dust
The city of LA
Los Angeles
The City of Angels
The angels?
I think not
We are more of the city of lost angeles
Our minds have advanced
We have advanced in a lot
LA has advanced from a nice vacation spot to a...
Big place, full of fears
A community
2 communities
3 communities
4 communities
9 communities
13 communities
A bunch of communities
Communities that could connect
Communities that could connect and change
Change LA completely
Bring it back to its nice vacation spot
But LA is LA
LA wants to be LA
LA has many things
LA is remorse
LA is my home
My home to come
My home that was.

PHILIPPA MCKEVITT, 6TH GRADE
NEW ROADS SCHOOL, LOS ANGELES COUNTY
ALEX RAND, CLASSROOM TEACHER
INDIA RADFAR, POET-TEACHER

The Marigold Sun

I have nightmares
of the golden sun
finishing its fall
a wilting marigold dying, sending final rays of weak sunshine
the flower I used to see sitting beside sugar skulls on an *ofrenda*
but it was then drenching the skyline in despair
backlighting the hunched bodies running across railroad tracks
the sundown I will forever remember
The marigold I will never forget
The feeling of drowning,
paddling as hard as you can, but yet never able to stay afloat
each breath further ensuring your demise
the hurried pitter-patter of rushed footsteps
of Papa clutching Mama's hand
Mama clutching my hand
Me clutching my worn *muñeca*
We are a chain of desperation, each of us a link held together by
hope
We wear somber expressions and holey clothing
We bring nothing but the clothes on our backs and the cries of the
familia
we must leave behind
the hope of generations of ancestors on our shoulders
I clamber aboard the train, stray nails sticking out of decrepit
crates
sinking into the shadows
and whispering prayers of hope that no eagle-eyed watchmen will
see us.
Then the short-lived sigh of relief when I hear the rhythmic
rumbling
of wheels churning against train tracks

knowing that this is only the beginning
I wake up from my nightmare by the time the train reaches San Diego.
I recall the rest of my story as I shrug off grogginess
remembering the struggle of being in a foreign land
hearing only gibberish when everyone else hears sentences
But then the painful but successful descent into American life.
Fathers teaching daughters to only marry white men
forcing integration into society none of us want a part of
Spanish becomes Spanglish becomes English
except behind our peeling closed doors
then, I can hear Mama whisper to Tia
in hushed Spanish
as if an immigration officer will appear
from behind the faded floral curtains
the language of home
of dry sand under my feet
of the smell of *bunuelos* crackling in the kitchen
of the hand painted ceramic pig banks
lovingly crafted, and with no hole in the bottom
you put everything in, yet get nothing out.
a twisted reminder for little Mexican children
so different from the cheap plastic ones here in America,
Now, I walk into the basement below Papa's store,
and take in a deep breath of flour and warmth and happiness
waving greetings to the workers elbow deep in dough
smiling when I hear the sizzle of *tortilla*
against scorching pan.
and there, in that magical tortilla-frying kitchen,
I can feel the sugary *conchas* dissolving on my tongue,
the heat of the marigold sun on my tanned skin,

the embraces of my *familia*,

the memories of Mexico.

I am home.

JAXI COHEN, 9TH GRADE
LOWELL HIGH SCHOOL, SAN FRANCISCO COUNTY
JENNIFER MOFFITT, CLASSROOM TEACHER
SUSAN TERENCE, POET-TEACHER

muñeca - doll
bunuelos - fried mexican cookie/donut/crepe
conchas - mexican sweet bread

IF POETRY WAS A COLOR

Poem Soda

Drink rich, sweet metaphors
slurp the cold sugary periods.
Don't be afraid to spill on verbs.
Dig your mouth into the brown liquid
in the cup's icy cold exclamation marks.
Never stop writing to get that
ice cold sugary adjective.
Don't be shy, do not be polite
dig right through your drink
to the bottom of the page.
Because some people want to
take everything away from you.
Don't let that happen.
Do whatever you want.
Don't be polite, be messy.
Don't listen to them.
Write about whatever you want
when you want.
I hope this inspires people
who want to become future poets.

CARLOS DUFFIELD, 4TH GRADE
PRESTWOOD ELEMENTARY, SONOMA COUNTY
SHANNON MCCAMBRIDGE, CLASSROOM TEACHER
SANDRA ANFANG, POET-TEACHER

Only a Poem

Only a poem knows
what's happening far out
in the deep dark space.
It's impossible to bring fear
inside the soul of a poem.
Poems are feelings
without negativeness.
Poems feel sad
when they're not focused on.
If an ocean gets lost in a poem
it becomes happiness.

CRUZ GATTNAR, 3RD GRADE
PARK ELEMENTARY, MARIN COUNTY
JOE MARTINI, CLASSROOM TEACHER
PRARTHO SERENO, POET-TEACHER

Mr. Pen

Mr. Minne gave me an eraser,
white and as fluffy as the
clouds.

It had been through a hurricane
of magic,
loved so much, with love.

It unlocked the authentic,
and covered the weird
like a piñata filled with wonder
and exploration with its own
story to tell.

Why is there yellow?
Only it knows.

Silence might be the cause
or his amazing texture,
his amazing name, Mr. Pen,
a blessing to the paper,
a blessing to the pencil,
Mr. Pen.

Oh, Mr. Pen.

ASHA NAYAK, 4TH GRADE
VIEJA VALLEY ELEMENTARY, SANTA BARBARA
ALEXA MANNION, CLASSROOM TEACHER
CIE GUMUCIO, POET-TEACHER

The Words of History

The snowflakes fall in the early light
as the polar bear gallivants across the bleak landscape.
The narwhals leap across the twisting waves
as it gargles, encased in the crust of stone.
The wind screams persistently, the whales dive
> Down
>> Down
>>> down
to the precious treasure.

It emits whispers and secrets,
it is like a cup full of words overflowing
into the dark empty space at the bottom of the sea.
The water starts to churn with letters
turning into words, turning into sentences,
turning into the secret of the Arctic.

Greta LaFemina, 3rd grade
Vallecito School, Calaveras County
Meryl Ellison, Classroom Teacher
Terri Glass, Poet-Teacher

Long and Short

Some poems are
very long but I'm
not very long. Just long
enough. So let's get on
with the poem.
Not all poems are long.
Yeah...I said it, poems
are short. In fact I'll
stop right now.

VICTORIA LEWIS, 5TH GRADE
NEW ROADS SCHOOL, LOS ANGELES COUNTY
JENNIFER CARTER, CLASSROOM TEACHER
INDIA RADFAR, POET-TEACHER

Bad Poem

My poems are
bad. My poems are
weak like a grass
blade. My poems are
gross and rotten like
slimy kale. My poems
are boring like bland
soup. My poems are
disappointing like
no dessert after dinner.

Finn Talley, 6th grade
McKinleyville Middle School, Humboldt County
Marcy Howe, Classroom Teacher
Dan Zev Levinson, Poet-Teacher

Not My Strong Suit
(a pantoum)

Poetry is not my strong suit
Poetry is like throwing myself
Off the roof
Or into a volcano

Poetry is like throwing myself
Out of a window
Or into a volcano
It is the equivalent of a nuke

Out of a window
Into a 4-way intersection
It is the equivalent of a nuke
On a Sunday

Into a 4-way intersection
Off the roof
On a Sunday
Poetry is not my strong suit

JAXON CRAIG, 6TH GRADE
MOUNTAIN VIEW ELEMENTARY, SANTA BARBARA COUNTY
KELLY HAMMOND, CLASSROOM TEACHER
RON ALEXANDER, POET-TEACHER

Tucked Away

Poems lurk in the corner of your mind
covered with cobwebs gathering dust
poems pitch a tent and light a fire
toasting marshmallows they wait.

They fall asleep to vivid dreams shattered
with twist and turns.
Poems wake to gears turning
as they leap out of the way
avoiding the thought train,
dream after dream they stay tucked away.

Poems with their nasal voice and tiny mouth
shout, "Remember me!"
The door creaks opens in your mind
as rusty as a 50-year-old can of unopened beans.

You can only find poems
down the river of emotions
riding the elevator of love down
straight to the depths of your heart.

CLARA WATSON, 5TH GRADE
MONTECITO UNION SCHOOL, SANTA BARBARA COUNTY
JUDY BRIGHTON, CLASSROOM TEACHER
LOIS KLEIN, POET-TEACHER

My Poem

My poem goes through a long journey.
Through the rainfalls and the valley.
A poem doesn't make one sound.
It makes many.
Poems are sorrowful, happy, mad, and kind.
My poem meets many people who are cruel and generous.
My poem is in the season of evergreen.
Evergreen, the tree that's green all year,
but can burn like a light switch.
My poem is made out of my emotions,
too confusing even for me.
My poem goes through a long journey.
My poem.

STEPHANIE URAGA, 6TH GRADE
JAMES MONROE ELEMENTARY, SONOMA COUNTY
NIKKI WINOVICH, CLASSROOM TEACHER
PHYLLIS MESHULAM, POET-TEACHER

The Book Was...

The book was a bird
The pages were the bones
It flew all over the class
The book flew in the library
The librarian chased the flying book
everywhere
and finally caught the book
Then put the book back
When the librarian left
the book flew out

ANDREA DIAZ, 4TH GRADE
MIRAMONTE ELEMENTARY SCHOOL, LOS ANGELES COUNTY
TOM LOUIE, CLASSROOM TEACHER
ALICE PERO, POET-TEACHER

Book

I am a book dropping. The kind
that can see the monsters in you. The one
book that can read you instead of you reading
it. I'm no original book perhaps I'm
not a book at all maybe I'm a dream. A musical
dream that doesn't play music at all. Or I'm
a wish that people have seen never before.
A wish that could fly away close my eyes
get lost in a secret place no one will find.

BAYLEE CARPENTER, 5TH GRADE
PENINSULA ELEMENTARY SCHOOL, HUMBOLDT COUNTY
TESS YINGER AND LINDA STEWART, CLASSROOM TEACHERS
DAN ZEV LEVINSON, POET-TEACHER

Books

Art—too expensive
Comics—too juvenile
Horror—too gory
Romance—too limited
Poetry—too personal
Cookbooks—too much sugar
Nonfiction—too real
Sci-Fi—too many robots
Drama—too repetitive
Fantasy—too over-the-top
Comedy—too happy
There's always more.
I love it all.

Elliot Abrahams, 6th grade
McKinleyville Middle School, Humboldt County
Marcy Howe, Classroom Teacher
Dan Zev Levinson, Poet-Teacher

If Poetry

If poetry was a color,
it would be tie-dye to represent
its mixed feelings.

If poetry was an animal,
it would be a falcon,
swooping for majestic words.

If poetry was a classroom,
it would teach outstanding words.

If poetry was a place,
it would be the marvelous ocean
where words drift through the sand.

If poetry could change the world,
it would prevent people
from using abstract words.

But the real magic of poetry
is what you do and make with it.

Seagrin Lawless, 4th grade
Spreckels Elementary, San Diego County
Deron Bear, Classroom Teacher
Celia Sigmon, Poet-Teacher

Feeling Colors

Blue sounds like wind blowing through my ears
Green sounds like March clovers getting ready for spring
When I'm angry, red fills my head
When I'm feeling sad, blue melts down my mind
And yellow is when I'm happy and fills me with joy

Avery Simington, 3rd grade
Delphi Academy, Los Angeles County
Ann Swapp, Classroom Teacher
Alice Pero, Poet-Teacher

Blue's Feelings

Blue sounds like a bird singing in a cherry tree.
It looks like a white cloud hanging over the city.
Blue tastes like a sweet juicy pear on a plate.
It smells like a small fluffy kitten on a doorstep,
meowing softly.
Blue feels like a poem being read.
It's the song of an orange fox in the forest.

LIVIA COREA, 1ST GRADE
STRAWBERRY POINT ELEMENTARY, MARIN COUNTY
ERIKA JENSEN, CLASSROOM TEACHER
PRARTHO SERENO, POET-TEACHER

Baby Blue

See what Baby Blue
can do. He is as cool
as a Lamborghini. He feels
like a diamond as tall as
a pyramid. He says he
is ready for another poem.
He is as calm as an
everyday time. He moves
like a cheetah getting its
food taken away. He tastes
like an ice cream sandwich.
Baby Blue wants to be
baby new. I wonder
what else Baby Blue
can do. Probably more than
you.

Davey Hipes, 2nd grade
Ambrosini Elementary School, Humboldt County
René Brown, Classroom Teacher
Dan Zev Levinson, Poet-Teacher

Sky and Sea

Blue is the color of the sky
The barrier to the black beyond
Blue is the color that blocks
The dark of the abyss at the
Bottom of the ocean
Blue is a raging storm, but it is also
A calm river flowing gently
Blue is big and broad, calm and gentle
Sky and sea
This is Blue
To me

FRITZ MOSS, 3RD GRADE
NEW ROADS SCHOOL, LOS ANGELES COUNTY
SHELLY FREDMAN-FETZER, CLASSROOM TEACHER
INDIA RADFAR, POET-TEACHER

Blue

Blue is like the ocean
Blue is as precious as a sapphire
Blue smells like a fresh blueberry
Blue sounds like a blue jay's sweet song
Blue looks like the summer sky
Blue feels like snow on a winter's day
Blue calms me as I sleep

CADENCE LU, 3RD GRADE
COLD SPRING SCHOOL, SANTA BARBARA COUNTY
BECKI GONZALEZ, CLASSROOM TEACHER
MEGAN YOUNG, POET-TEACHER

Black

Oh black,
you pull out the skies with your inky darkness.
You are the darkness that makes
the stars gleam when I am in bed.
You are the night.
You are the entrance of a bear's cave.
You are the crow who will swoop down to eat his lunch.
You are what's left of a dead rose.
You are the ashes of a great man who changed America.

COLTON SCHAEFER, 3RD GRADE
VALLECITO SCHOOL, MARIN COUNTY
MERYL ELINSON, CLASSROOM TEACHER
TERRI GLASS, POET-TEACHER

Red in Music

A cloud it is red
There is a piano there, a little cloud, a mist
the mist floats near the piano and it starts playing
The piano and the soft melody
then the mist goes to the drum
It starts bouncing on the drum
and makes a tune
Then it goes to the flute
It plays the flute
Then it goes to the guitar and strums
The mist cloud plays all of the instruments
And it makes red in music

Edward Lopez, 4th grade
Miramonte Elementary School, Los Angeles County
Tom Louie, Classroom Teacher
Alice Pero, Poet-Teacher

Gold

Gold is always first.
Why can't gold be third?
Maybe sometimes
gold doesn't want
to compete in
races. Maybe gold
wants to work
in a salon, or
a restaurant? Maybe
gold doesn't want
to stand out
and be sparkly.
Maybe gold doesn't
want to have all
the attention. Gold
is probably sorry
for Bronze and
Silver. Gold is probably
shy, not snobby,
and scared, not brave.
But this is how
it has to go.

Elana Rowan, 5th grade
Cold Spring Elementary, Santa Barbara County
Linda Edwards, Classroom Teacher
Ron Alexander, Poet-Teacher

Ode to Brown

you are forgotten, misunderstood
you are real nature. not green
you are real happiness, not yellow
when people think of you they
think of lazy mud that sits around, not
soil, the mother of all life.

Kacy Truc-Vy Kramer, 5th grade
Summerland School, Santa Barbara County
Nichole Hughes, Classroom Teacher
Lalli Dana Drobny, Poet-Teacher

Blue's Lament

When winter receded
and white went to rest;
when spring came
and the sky emerged,
Blue was reborn—cold but shy.

He shook hands with Green
with Brown and with Gold.
None seemed to mind that
he was so cold.

He walked away swiftly
and joined the waves.
When night was bestowed upon him,
he greeted the stars,
he high-fived the moon,
he waved "hi" to Mars.

He sang his sad song of
confusion, yet balance.
He watched as Black emerged below.
He is the opposite of Orange—
happy and joyful and bouncy
and fun.

He wears a mask of feelings
to hide his apathy.
He made his wish to the clouds,
the only white left.

AKASHA BOWEN, 5TH GRADE
APPLE BLOSSOM ELEMENTARY SCHOOL, SONOMA COUNTY
DYLAN LICCIARDO, CLASSROOM TEACHER
JACKIE HUSS HALLERBERG, POET-TEACHER

Gypsy Caravan Turquoise

When I see the sky it reminds me
  of Gypsy Caravan.
Sometimes I just smell something beautiful
  and then I think of Gypsy Caravan.
Gypsy Caravan reminds me of a special
  spice that has not been recounted.
Gypsy Caravan reminds me of a turquoise rock.
Gypsy Caravan reminds me of my best friend
  and me together holding hands and watching
  the sunset.
Gypsy Caravan reminds me of scuba diving
  in the deep blue sea.
Gypsy Caravan is an emotion of sadness.
Gypsy Caravan is the color of Neptune and
  its big blue dot.
Gypsy Caravan is my color and I love it.

Gemma Geldert, 3rd grade
Prestwood Elementary School, Sonoma County
Carly Costello, Classroom Teacher
Sandra Anfang, Poet-Teacher

A Blessing to the Paper
~Ekphrastic Poems~

The Jimson Weed
(after a Georgia O'Keefe painting)

I.

I am the son of heaven.
The comet of the soil.
The glistening bittersweet fruit of the earth.
The blanket of the stars.
I am the gold of the Milky Way.
The tree of heaven.
The Northern Lights.
The Father of humanity.
The spiral of life.

II.

I am a dove soaring
at dusk among
the sequoias and cedars
Like a violin playing
on its silky strings
Like a piano playing
a sonata at dawn.

KIRAN THOLE, 3RD GRADE
FRANCIS SCOTT KEY ELEMENTARY SCHOOL
SAN FRANCISCO COUNTY
MAY CHUNG, CLASSROOM TEACHER
SUSAN TERENCE, POET-TEACHER

Mexico

(after a painting)

In the patio of the Mexican restaurant
there's a flowing water fountain
with plants all around it.
There's a blue chair with a guitar.
The walls are painted like a serape—
red, yellow, purple, blue and white.

I'm the guitar lying on the chair.
I start to move and my strings quiver
when I hear the water fountain splashing.
When I play a tune, the red roses
grow taller, reaching to touch me.

Zana Schreier, 3rd grade
Spreckels Elementary, San Diego County
Marisela Sparks, Classroom Teacher
Seretta Martin, Poet-Teacher

The Grand Canyon
(after a photo)

I'm at the colossal canyon.
It reminds me of when I flew over
the Grand Canyon in a helicopter,
but now I'm actually here on the cliff
looking down.

The air smells like fresh berries.
Lizards crawl and creatures roam.
There's orange rocks and white flowers.
A few green plants grow out of cracks
in the steep rocks.

The lizards are playing tag and
snakes are racing with each other.
Now the lizards are like kids having a race
and the snakes are having Snake Olympics.

PARKER RICHARDSON, 3RD GRADE
SPRECKELS ELEMENTARY SCHOOL, SAN DIEGO COUNTY
MILLIE WEIL, CLASSROOM TEACHER
SERETTA MARTIN, POET-TEACHER

A Couple Dining Midair

(after a Korean Air flight ad)

How are they sitting outside
on the airplane's wing
and how is the food not flying away?

In the strong wind, how are the candles
not blowing out and how did they
sneak past the flight attendant?

Just how are they not sliding off the airplane?

I'm the man on the wing and I know
how we stayed there.
Believe, and you're half way there.

TUCKER WOJDOWSKI, 3RD GRADE
SPRECKELS ELEMENTARY SCHOOL, SAN DIEGO COUNTY
MICHAEL FRENCH, CLASSROOM TEACHER
SERETTA MARTIN, POET-TEACHER

The Tree
(after Vincent Van Gogh's painting, the "Mulberry Tree")

The tree
fire burning
leaves
has no love nor heart
nobody to give
him water
the burning leaves are like you
with your burning desire
to win
the dark blue sky
bigger than the ocean but
not your
heart
the tree feels sadness
and wishes to
be reborn like a phoenix
the tree is burning
like a grill… but no
it is a tree.

BEN STONE, 4TH GRADE
POINSETTIA ELEMENTARY, VENTURA COUNTY
DIANE SATHER AND JULIE SOSKE, CLASSROOM TEACHERS
JENNIFER KELLEY, POET-TEACHER

Autumn Fire Tree
(after Vincent Van Gogh's painting, the "Mulberry Tree")

The colorful Autumn tree
With all of its joyful leaves
And the cozy feeling of the fiery branches
Just like a fireplace where you can hear people talking
But what are they saying?
Friends reacquainted

Wyatt Mesker, 4th grade
Poinsettia Elementary, Ventura County
Diane Sather and Julie Soske, Classroom Teachers
Jennifer Kelley, Poet-Teacher

Spotted Dog
(after a photo)

Wednesday night I snuck into the church
when I heard singing and I started howling
and whipping the piano with my tail.
There were sirens outside, but
I kept howling louder. Everyone was singing.
Then my owner, a little girl in a white dress,
lacy cap and white shoes, jumped in front
of the audience and started to sing. I was still
whipping the piano and howling
as we sang louder than the sirens.
Everyone said we sang so well!
How surprised we were when they invited us
to come sing every Wednesday night.
I am the happiest spotted dog in the world.

KYLIE PETERSON, 4TH GRADE
BANYAN TREE LEARNING CENTER, SAN DIEGO COUNTY
TANYA SUTTON, CLASSROOM TEACHER
SERETTA MARTIN, POET-TEACHER

Brussels Sprouts
(after William Blake's, "The Tyger")

Brussels sprouts, why do you taste gross?

My uncle said I had to.

Brussels sprouts, how are you healthy?

It's the law.

Brussels sprouts, why do you torture kids?

It suits me.

CADE MOHARRAM, 4TH GRADE
PEABODY CHARTER SCHOOL, SANTA BARBARA COUNTY
LINDA STIRLING, CLASSROOM TEACHER
RON ALEXANDER, POET-TEACHER

Chagall

I see a man and a woman dancing in the air,
the toxic proximity propelled them up there.
The woman is joyful, that man is very keen.
They fly over the town as they dip in the air
as a bird with giant wings.
They start to stop dancing in a shimmer of light,
They land on the ground with the memory
of first kiss and its burden of flight.

BRITTA THORNAL, 4TH GRADE
CLAIRE LILIENTHAL SCHOOL, SAN FRANCISCO COUNTY
MS. CARRILLO, CLASSROOM TEACHER
GAIL NEWMAN, POET-TEACHER

Suzanne Collins

Suzanne Collins is like a
blowing teapot of ideas. Her
books are not for 1 hour
reading. It takes days to read
The Hunger Games.
She acts like a racer that won't stop
till they blow that whistle as
loud as a kitchen cabinet slamming
shut. Her hair is like yellow mustard
and her skin is like whitish burger bun.

JAKE WEDEMEYER, 4TH GRADE
CLAIRE LILIENTHAL SCHOOL, SAN FRANCISCO COUNTY
MS. ELLERS, CLASSROOM TEACHER
GAIL NEWMAN, POET-TEACHER

The Great Wave Haiku
(after the painting by Kiyoshi Otsuka)

Three boats leave mountain
because tsunami breaks them
like a broken heart.

JOSUE MUÑOZ, 4TH GRADE
BAHIA VISTA ELEMENTARY, MARIN COUNTY
COLIN JOHNSON, CLASSROOM TEACHER
LEA ASCHKENAS, POET-TEACHER

The Persistence of Memory
(after the Salvador Dali painting)

A lumber-made shelf,
a tree branch with a
clock spreading larger.

Morning sky water-colored
with a river and shelter,
an area with shade.

Three clocks with the same time
to keep the memory alive.

Myrna Escamilla, 4th grade
Bahia Vista Elementary, Marin County
Colin Johnson, Classroom Teacher
Lea Aschkenas, Poet-Teacher

Cape Cod Morning
(after a painting by Edward Hopper)

Lonely, without her dog
to pet, to feed, to love.
Now a lonely stray without love.
No Purina dog chow
in the crisp clean morning.
Looking and waiting
for him to maybe come back.
She thinks:
"I bet the dog misses the smell
of my blueberry pancakes
and my nice cool hands
giving him a belly rub.
I just wish I could get
my best friend back."

NICO INGARGIOLA, 5TH GRADE
OLIVE ELEMENTARY, MARIN COUNTY
FRAN ROZOFF, CLASSROOM TEACHER
LEA ASCHKENAS, POET-TEACHER

On the Other Side of the Painting

On the other side of the painting
There may be a great island
With mountains as tall as giants.

On the other side of the painting
There may be an obstacle greater than yourself
There may be the moon with bright intentions.

On the other side of the painting
There may be a forest with never ending trees
But you'll never know if you don't pick up the paintbrush.

JOCELYN COULTRÉ, 5TH GRADE
APPLE BLOSSOM SCHOOL, SONOMA COUNTY
DYLAN LICCIARDO, CLASSROOM TEACHER
LISA SHULMAN, POET-TEACHER

Lightning Bolt

(inspired by a Layne Kennedy photo)

Just as the lightning makes a strike.
I like to think that I'm that grey cloud.
I close my eyes and think how it feels like.
All these colors go to my mind.
Blue, grey, and purple too. More colors.
I think I'm sinking, then POP.
I'm a lightning bolt.
Boom, boom!
I open my eyes and it's all gone.
Just imagining it makes it fun!

ARIANNA RAMOS, 4TH GRADE
DANA GRAY ELEMENTARY SCHOOL, MENDOCINO COUNTY
LYNETTE MAY, CLASSROOM TEACHER
KAREN LEWIS, POET-TEACHER

My Compass Doesn't Do
What a Compass Does

My Weird Compass

My compass doesn't do what a compass does
My compass shows me where
my heart wants to go
My compass can be very
inconvenient
My compass can be very annoying
Why does my compass act this way?

SYLVIA HARSH, 5TH GRADE
MENDOCINO K-8 ELEMENTARY, MENDOCINO COUNTY
JOHN MORAN, CLASSROOM TEACHER
HUNTER GAGNON, POET-TEACHER

The Museum of Broken Things

Broken dreams, wishes, and hopes:
the things we can feel but are invisible to the naked eye.

The dreams of inventing something amazing and new
broken and crushed by the people who say you can't and you won't.

The wishes of a dog sink into the void of reality
like nobody ever knew it was even there.

The hopes of your life following the right path,
but then it takes the wrong turn.

The unraveled scarf of the wind,
from a storm too big for it to handle.

The broken pencil that danced of the first word
then gave up without ever trying again.

The rotten apple thrown at the unwanted guest,
because they said it impossible.

The umbrella that thought it could protect its person,
second guessed itself and rode the wind away.

The eraser smudge with the lead of a pencil split into four parts
for friends to share when it wanted to stay together.

The museum of broken things is a fraction of our imagination
that we made up to fill the empty space between us.

SARAH KEMPER, 4TH GRADE
OLD MILL SCHOOL, MARIN COUNTY
KAREN LEVIN, CLASSROOM TEACHER
TERRI GLASS, POET-TEACHER

Green Shirt

your green print
like an old lady on
a grass field. used
accepted happy about
your days spent. picture
after picture, year
after year. appreciated.
   you
     a
      r
       e
          m
           y
  shirt.

forever.
(or at least until
middle school)

but still you should
dance in my closet
like a ballerina and
glow like an emerald.

Massimo Bonilla-Zakosek, 5th grade
Summerland School, Santa Barbara County
Nichole Hughes, Classroom Teacher
Lalli Dana Drobny, Poet-Teacher

To My Braces

Thank you!
Okay, so yes,
You are very painful sometimes,
And you do stop me from some things,
But I do want to thank you,
I want to thank you in the long run,
The run of my life, longer than a marathon.
Right now you are still on my teeth,
You are making them straight, like a line, a perfect line.

You have helped me not eat vegetables (don't tell mom and dad),
Even though I do really like vegetables, but not always.
You have made me not eat candy, but I can live with that,

I like choosing your colors, any colors I want.
Colors against your shiny metal, metal that changes me.
You can make my mouth feel like it has been cut in every place,
and when I like you the best,
you feel like nothing, nothing at all.
My sometimes painful, sometimes ruining my smile
and my sometimes friend,
Thank you, your gonna be great in the long run (I hope).

Hazel Heckes, 6th grade
Roosevelt Elementary School, Santa Barbara
Barbara Barr, Classroom Teacher
Lalli Dana Drobny, Poet-Teacher

Sounds like...

In cereal the milk when you pour it
sounds like rain dripping on my head
It also sounds like someone
tapping on my window
trying to talk to me

AVERY SIMINGTON, 3RD GRADE
DELPHI ACADEMY, LOS ANGELES COUNTY
ANN SWAPP, CLASSROOM TEACHER
ALICE PERO, POET-TEACHER

The Flattest Thing

The flattest thing in the world
is a pancake.
It is golden like the sun
dazzling in the sky.
It sounds like an egg
sizzling in a pan
and looks like a circle saying
"Please eat me!
I'm really yummy!"
It feels like an edible pillow
drizzled with syrup.
It can take you to
a whole different world!

LAWLER JACKSON, 2ND GRADE
MONTECITO UNION SCHOOL, SANTA BARBARA COUNTY
DR. JUDY COMPTON, CLASSROOM TEACHER
LOIS KLEIN, POET-TEACHER

The Tea Book

Ladies drink tea.
They stick their
pinky up and
take a tiny, tiny
tiny sip and
put it down on their
old plate. Then they
take their napkin and tap their lips
gently.

DELIA MOSS, 2ND GRADE
NEW ROADS SCHOOL, LOS ANGELES COUNTY
JENNIFER CARTER, CLASSROOM TEACHER
INDIA RADFAR, POET-TEACHER

Ode to the Garbage Can

You're filled to the rim
like a too-full cup,
spilling over the sides,
and I have to pick you up.
What could be crawling
In your depths?
Rolly pollies? Pincher bugs?
Your stench could cause
quick deaths. And
at night when the
raccoons creep,
the smell makes
even the vultures weep.

ADDISON EVERAGE, 5TH GRADE
TAM VALLEY ELEMENTARY, MARIN COUNTY
ROBIN ALDERSON, CLASSROOM TEACHER
LEA ASCHKENAS, POET-TEACHER

Quotidian Cube

Cold and clear with sharply cut corners
A perfect—no
A correct cube
Other than the small shard-shaped hole
On the right side of the side most often to my right

There are faces on the other sides
I see them clearly as they do me
They speak amongst themselves
Chittering and chattering
With the occasional remark thrown my way
I watch the frantic movements of their dry, parched lips
Cracked from the long and sustained dehydration
But I cannot hear their varied voices
Leaving me to guess at the meanings
Their ever evolving ovular embouchures
Are attempting to convey

I answer back, feeling silly as I do
For pretending that the clear barriers
Which I see so clearly
Do not restrict my earnestly answering voice

But maybe I'll get lucky and one will watch my lips
And bother to look for meaning

Nevertheless, tomorrow I will try again
The crisis evolving and devolving
Like the sun rising and falling

Me screaming out, them glancing in

And the glass box between us
To hold it all in place

The same colorless bodies keeping position
The same heart beating with desperation

GEORGIA SCHREINER, 11TH GRADE
VILLANOVA PREPARATORY SCHOOL, VENTURA COUNTY
JULIE HEDRICK, CLASSROOM TEACHER
FERNANDO SALINAS, POET-TEACHER

A Violin

There was a box and
in the box was a red violin
that had two "L" holes,
eighty-one strings and when it played
it was the music of a poem
and for the bow
it had a hundred hairs of a fox

ORION GAINSFORTH, 3RD GRADE
DELPHI ACADEMY, LOS ANGELES COUNTY
GRANT YOUN, CLASSROOM TEACHER
ALICE PERO, POET-TEACHER

The Life of Music

Silky, soft, loving hands
tap

    tap

        TAP
against a drum
making a sound so beautiful

When you hear the sound
it makes you dance
knowing that love is possible

When the song stops
the hands shine but
start to dance with glee
These hands have a future as open
as a land filled with music

The town will sing and dance
when the drum beats again,
having fun, laughter and loving WHEEs

MADISON REAGAN LEEDY, 3RD GRADE
RICHARD BARD ELEMENTARY, VENTURA COUNTY
NADEAN SANCHEZ NAJARA, CLASSROOM TEACHER
FERNANDO SALINAS, POET-TEACHER

To Make an Orchestra

Lightly simmer the whispers.
Crack open the curtain. Pour to the side.
Shake in the rustles of preparation.
Sprinkle in the coughs to the whispers.
Bring to a broil.
When the suspense bubbles up, begin the main dish.
Chop up the brassy notes of a trumpet.
Thaw the baritones. Stir in slowly.
Blend the violins into the mix.
Wash the drums before adding.
Stir when clean.
Frost with flutes and sprinkle with piccolos.
Cool with the breeze of the cellos.
Cut into bite-size pieces.
Serve on a platter on the table of the stage.
Pour the curtains over it as a garnish.

UMA ANANDAKUTTAN, 5TH GRADE
APPLE BLOSSOM ELEMENTARY SCHOOL, SONOMA COUNTY
JEANNE GUERINONI, CLASSROOM TEACHER
JACKIE HUSS HALLERBERG, POET-TEACHER

Origin of Tennis

Tennis
is a mixture
of three gods
Baseball's idea
of hitting a ball
Basketball's hoop
yet with a handle
A spider's web
Criss-cross criss-cross criss-cross
'Til the end of time
All these sports
Entwined
to make
the best sport of all
The overpowering goddess
Tennis

Delilah Rain Sheehan, 5th grade
West Marin School, Marin County
Esther Underwood, Classroom Teacher
Brian Kirven, Poet-Teacher

Opposites

On the other side of the lion there is freedom.

On the other side of hate is kindness.

On the other side of left is right.

On the other side of greed is faith.

On the other side of rain is sun.

On the other side of death there is birth.

On the other side of anticipation is excitement.

On the other side of closed there is opened.

On the other side of discouragement there is inspiration.

On the other side of horrible is amazing.

On the other side of tiny is vast.

On the other side of fast there is slow.

On the other side of break there is build.

On the other side of cold is warm.

On the other side of empty is full.

CLAYTON HUNTER, 5TH GRADE
MENDOCINO K-8 ELEMENTARY, MENDOCINO COUNTY
JOHN MORAN, CLASSROOM TEACHER
KAREN LEWIS AND HUNTER GAGNON, POET-TEACHERS

A Way of Life
That Only the Stars Understand

~Poet-Teacher Poems~

Backyard Vista of the Bird Fiesta

Ascend
Descend the Golden-crowned Sparrow,
the Oregon Junco, the White-breasted Nuthatch.
Surprise my eye oh Spotted Towhee
Descend the rain, the roots of oak.

Walk on down to the rising river
Way beyond the railroad tracks
Quack the Mallard in the slough
And a V of Canvasback swims into view.

Ascend
Descend the California Towhee,
the Oak Titmouse, the White-crowned Sparrow.
Flit like a fly you skittish House Finch,
Tip the birdfeeder bully Scrub Jay,
Descend the rain, the roots of oak.

Tromp my boots to the muddy hillside
Find windswept branches strewn about
Whistle the robin in her habitat
while an Acorn Woodpecker rat a tat tats.

Ascend
Descend the Chestnut-backed Chickadee,
the Downy Woodpecker and Mockingbird.
Scratch the leaf litter little Fox Sparrow,
Hang upside down you crazy nuthatch,
Scatter, zigzag, wild bird fiesta
Rejoice this winter solstice.

TERRI GLASS, POET-TEACHER

MARIN COUNTY

Cross-Pollination
—inspired by Federico García Lorca's "La luna asoma"

The full moon peaks through
the school yard Monterey pines
where I will teach tomorrow
on sense and color fusion
in translation.

The swinging bulbs
of windblown hall lights
leave an orange blur
and a hint of citrus
wafts across the world

like the second grader Max
had reported tasting orange peels
from miles away, the perfume
brought in on the breeze.

Orange moon hovers
over gradual rolling slope line,
signature of this land,
and towers above jagged Sierra Nevada
over Lorca's Granada.

Even though he himself said
that "no one eats oranges,
only stone-cold green fruit
under the full moon,"
each packs its own sweetness,
roundness reflected in the bright
lantern of the night.

BRIAN KIRVEN, POET-TEACHER

MARIN COUNTY

Rayo Verde

¿Qué es el rayo verde
sino el beso
de amarillo y azul
en el matrimonio
del sol y la mar?

Green Flash

What is the green flash
but the kiss
of yellow and blue
in the marriage
of the sun and the sea?

BRIAN KIRVEN, POET-TEACHER
MARIN COUNTY

Beach Run

Stripped of her stories, she ran along the beach
running on rags and lumps left by merpeople,
dragging strings of green, popping iridescent bubbles
under her feet
The wind knew what she would say next and snatched
a long string of words, leaving her sea-bare, worn and polished
She wrapped slimy green seaweeds around slim limbs,
knocked the wind down,
walked silently through a pool of sun-drops,
gathered strands of words into a bucket
mixed with sand dollars, hermit crabs, gnarly starfish, pebbles,
bottle caps, echoes in a conch shell
They jingled and jangled, banged against her ankles,
Grains of sand fell
Stories flew into the air
She snatched them like kite strings, then
she let them go

Alice Pero, Poet-Teacher
Los Angeles County

Grand Canyon

Vast   the space between two facing rims,
the distance between our desires:

You need your pencil sharpened,
I need
my dad back.   here.
on this blue and green earth

I stand on the North,
squint to see you
away,
far away
on the South

bands of red rock like
layers of need
rise, plateau
rugged, remote
like our hearts

how do I order these needs,
these separate edges

if it doesn't get sharpened,
if he doesn't come back,
we might both

    T
       O
          P
             P
        L
          E

so here you go, little one:
your pencil, ready to use

but how will you bring me my father?

perhaps if I close my eyes
I can sharpen the image of his smiling face,
once more

MEGAN YOUNG, POET-TEACHER
SANTA BARBARA COUNTY

Blessing for the Laguna de Santa Rosa Trail
—*after Gary Snyder's "Prayer for the Great Family"*

Thanks be to the path, for its well-packed brown dirt,
leading me from one end to the other, gravel crunching beneath
as I walk this trail again and again
oh, to honor our earth this way.

Thanks be to the bench where I can rest, tie my boots,
make a sketch, write the lines to this poem
reflect on my life
oh, to honor our earth this way.

Thanks be to the gopher snake drawing out my breath,
giving my body a start, a shudder, then relief
as he slithers into the tall marsh grass
oh, to honor our earth this way.

Thanks be to the egrets, standing alone or in pairs,
then suddenly lifting off into cloudy skies, their flash of white
raising my eyes and my spirits
oh, to honor our earth this way.

Thanks be to the people I pass, our quick exchange of kind words
our common bond, sweetening this temporary stay
filled with entreaties and fragile hopes
oh, to honor our earth this way.

Thanks be to the generosity of nature and man,
to those who have reclaimed this land, planted themselves here,
survived for generations now and to come
oh, how we are honored to be among you.

Jackie Huss Hallerberg, Poet-Teacher
Sonoma County

Note: The Laguna de Santa Rosa trail is located off Occidental Road in Santa Rosa, California, and is part of a 22-mile-long wetland complex that drains a 254-square-mile watershed encompassing most of the Santa Rosa Plain in Sonoma County.

Daughter

Let us start on a grassy hill
overlooking the stars
where lovers intertwined
for the first time.

There will be years
to get to know each other
starting with the nine month journey.
The river will guide us

all the way to your crib
with a dream mobile
floating overhead.
Your father will be there.

We will hold your small hand
touch your hair
and see the miracle
of your chubby smile.

I can no longer tell
where the desire began
but I know it's been a lifetime
living without you.

SERETTA MARTIN, POET-TEACHER
SAN DIEGO COUNTY

In My Daughter's House

at Passover 2018

The yellow curtains in this guest room
are so bright that when I awake, or re-enter,
I am sure I have left a light on
or one has been left on for me—a lapse,
or a beacon?
　　　Outside, the trees are primed
for spring, sensing it in their bones,
their lovely carved bark, Escheresque
in its complexity. Their brown branches
and twigs criss-cross the gray sky,
seeking sunlight which surely lurks
just behind the thin layer of clouds.
And birds call to each other, tentative,
plaintive, asking, *Is it now?*
Is it soon? Spring? Yesterday, gold
flowed from the sky.
And I cry out, "Oh, let
my darling find her calling. Know
for herself what I can see—the warmth
of her kitchen, her home opened to friends
and poems and stories of deliverance.
Her dances with the dog, song sung for dogs,
her shoes competent and dancy, her heart
open to the afflicted, wine of the ages
ripe in her veins. Let her savor this syrup
boiled to acceptable thickness, then drenching
this cake made of the meal of the unleavened
bread of affliction. Let her discover
her balance, her voice,
　　　her beacon."

PHYLLIS MESHULAM, POET-TEACHER

SONOMA COUNTY

Ninguno Menos Rosa/None Less a Rose

(Poema de respuesta/Response poem)

Hay de negro y de blanco.
There are black and there are white.
De amarillo y coloradas tambien.
Yellow as well as red.
Ninguna menos rosa,
NONE LESS A ROSE,
menos humana que la otra,
less human than the rest.
Algunos damos fruto.
Some of us bear fruit.
Otros no.
Others, no.
Todos echamos flor.
Everyone blossoms.
Ninuguno menos rosa.
NONE LESS A ROSE.
De los que dan culto
of those who pray,
algunos se arrodillan manos dobladas,
some kneel hands folded.
Otros de pie con los brazos elevados.
Others stand, arms raised.
Ninguno menos rosa.
NONE LESS A ROSE.
Hay los que siguen la palabra calladitos.
There are those who silent listen.
Y otros que la declaman en voz alta.
And others that repeat the word out loud.

Muchos cantan.
Many sing.
Ninguno menos rosa.
NONE LESS A ROSE.
Me cuento con los plumados
   que bailan cara al sol.
I count myself with those who feathered dance
   face turned toward the sun.
¿Al Creador, quien le guste mas?
Who pleases the Creator most?
Buen padre siempre contesta:
A good father always replies:
"¡Tu, mi hijo!" "¡Mi hija, tu!"
"You, my son!" "My daughter, you!"
Ninguno menos rosa.
NONE LESS A ROSE.

JABEZ CHURCHILL, POET-TEACHER
MENDOCINO COUNTY

Playing With Dolls

Back then, we girls loved dolls: Barbies,
babies, changeable face ones that cried, smiled
or slept when we turned rubber knobs
on their painted hair heads
Each stunningly attired in cherished outfits:
silky bridal gowns with lacy cuffs,
tiny seed pearls on miniature
sleeves or flannel nighties floating
with smiling yellow ducks
Clearly, the boys in the family
missed out with their drab gray
and green plastic soldiers
and dull metal trucks until
the Christmas brother Tom opened
the package with his first GI Joe–
GI Joe with his flashy navy dress blues
and jaunty camouflage fatigues
prepared with doll sized M-16
to annihilate enemies in the brush–
a "super hero" model for boys
that perhaps foreshadowed Tom's later hobby:
collecting statues of sinister looking gnomes
and recently a man sized nutcracker
to guard his front door from Christmas thieves–
At six foot four, my sixty-year-old brother,
former basketball star and middle school
math teacher, still plays with what
looks an awfully lot
like dolls

CLAIRE BLOTTER, POET-TEACHER
MARIN COUNTY

Bounty

our childhood never leaves us
on my drive home
two dogwood trees
dazzling alabaster cups of joy
trumpet their greeting to me
I recall my mother's passion for dogwoods

I learned to love nature with her

our treks to Michigan blueberry fields
the blue Maxwell House coffee can
hanging around my neck on white string
I choose the biggest berries
eat most of them

fingers and mouth blue with glory
we bring home cornucopious buckets of them
mother makes packets of berries
for the big white freezer in the basement

our autumn harvests
nectarous aroma of Golden Delicious
crimson Rome Beauties and our favorite
crisp white Macintosh
in their bright red jackets
bushel baskets brimming with apples

we wrap each apple in crinkly newspaper
stow them in three shiny metal trash cans
with wide lids and broad handles

woosh
as we close each lid
on cans full of fall fruit

BETH BEURKENS, POET-TEACHER
SISKIYOU COUNTY

A Visit with Grandma

Follow me to the Bronx
where your feet slip
over the hard cobblestones of Fordham Road.
Cut through the tiny triangle of park
where old men feed cracker meal to pigeons.
Listen to the whipping of their startled wings
as they fly into morning sun
their breasts a rainbow of magenta and green.
Walk on until the smell of lollipops
and sugar cones tantalizes your nostrils.
You've come to Mr. Curran's candy store.
Turn clockwise, walk across the road
where the tall brown building looms
casts shadows on the freshly laundered sheets
that wave from fire escapes.
Listen for the crack of the wooden stick
against the leather ball
as children run bases in the street.
See their younger siblings play tag in the bare dirt lot.
Climb the creaky staircase with the rough green walls.
Knock on 3-C and there you'll find me
playing with my clothespin soldiers
on Grandma's kitchen floor.

SANDRA ANFANG, POET-TEACHER
SONOMA COUNTY

I Live Extreme

I live extreme
I live.
On,
To dream my grandfather's aspirations.
To fund my daughter's education.
On,
On,
To tend to the loneliest corner.
On,
To welcome my husband's kisses.
On,
To face my shadow as it revolves, past, present, future.
On, always leaving memories.

JESSICA M. WILSON, POET-TEACHER
LOS ANGELES COUNTY

Evangelio

No hay dioses cultos
ni incultos.
Ni buenos
ni malos
ni oscuros
ni claros,
solo la noche eterna y estrellada.
Su halito,
nieve y resina conifera,
destilado de la creacion,
condensado encima de parabrisas
y paragolpes igual
esperando un dedo infantil
que le trace sus nombres sinnumero
y el sol
a borrarselos.

Gospel

There are no tame
no wild gods.
No good,
no bad,
no dark,
no light,
just eternal starlit night.
It's breath,
pine pitch and snow,
clear distillate of creation,
condensed frozen upon windshields

and bumpers alike,
waiting for the finger of a child,
to trace its countless names,
and the sun
to be erased.

JABEZ W. CHURCHILL, POET-TEACHER
MENDOCINO COUNTY

Mice

Can you write a poem
In a storm,
In a frying pan,
Among the broken
Dropped like hail
Forgotten
Eaten to disrepair?
Can you do the thing
In a hurtful quiet
Through a pitiful rainfall
In a blur of lost language?
Can you write it full
And fearful
Desperate & stumbling?
Can you stoop
To create it?
Can you grow it
Like your mother did
Your name?
Can you wish it
When there are no stars
And the cool dark
Only holds mice
Trying to get in?

AMANDA CHIADO, POET-TEACHER
SAN BENITO COUNTY

The Happy Poem

When I am mad I am a mountain
When I am sad I am the wind
When I am happy I am a poem
Asking you to be my friend.

AMANDA CHIADO, POET-TEACHER
SAN BENITO COUNTY

Writer's Workshop Haiku

The lazy in me
wants you to say it's perfect
no need to revise.

LISA SHULMAN, POET-TEACHER
SONOMA COUNTY

On Reading Poetry in Tight Spaces

I am not someone you want in your parlor—
perched on a spindly satin covered chair
ankles crossed
knees pressed
together
eggshell china teacup
held hot to lips that sip—
I am not that person.

Nor do you want me
in your narrow art gallery
threading my way to a podium
past porcelain and glass balanced
and gleaming against egg white walls.

I come from a loud line
of arm wavers
and knee jigglers,
coffee sloshing in chipped mugs
slurped into mouths already full
and still talking
spewing cake crumbs
and bad news.

My words are not tame
enough for those places
they blare and bump
and burst their seams;
they snort and snicker,
gallop up and down
the shocked space

getting mud on the floor
and sticky fingerprints on the walls
before exploding out the door
in a wild splatter
of color and sound
scattering in the streets
like drunken friends
finding their way home.

LISA SHULMAN, POET-TEACHER
SONOMA COUNTY

Out Loud

this afternoon, I walked through my garden
as each blossom I'd cared for stretched
wingspan of their petals & began reciting
the words we'd practiced all winter,
waiting for spring

the lily mourned for Annabel Lee

the violet found the woods lovely, dark and deep

the sunflower cried, I am Ozymandius!

the daffodil slayed the Jabberwocky

the rose did not go gentle—

I'm sure there are gardeners who suffice
in silent greenhouses, quiet thoughts
filling their planter boxes of dark soil,

but I've never been more proud moving
words and earth until planted seeds
stand in the full bloom of poetry
as though it were no less necessary
than sunlight

Brennan DeFrisco, Poet-Teacher
Alameda County

how poems spring to life

one student trots then gallops into story
races through three pages long before
neighbor's
pencil is
out
the gate

another's eyes squint
close tight
open bright
remembering precise
slight
scent of blue eyed grass framed by pink yellow sky

some poets draw pictures
point arrows
cross out
write over
hum sing
tap fingers   toes   forehead
chin

begin
again

one resists
why should I?
you can't   don't make
          me
write a poem not about me

I'm tired
want sleep not more bore
boreboringschool rules
justletmeplay fortnight

finally week five fortnitefortnitefornite
finds—with table mates
perfect title for first
                        favorite
    soft   slow   cat
poem:
"sly"
    above it writes:
please type

LALLI DANA DROBNY, POET-TEACHER
SANTA BARBARA COUNTY

Did the Flower Know

(inspired by a pastel drawing)

Did the flower know
   what it would be
      when, as a swirl,
         it began?

Was it a thought
   in God's mind?
      Or simply the swish
         of a hand?

Were the petals
   a plan from the start?
      Or did they unfold
         over time?

Did moon or music
   soothe their hearts
      until their light
         could shine?

Perhaps this
   is the gift
      of pastels,
         petals,
           and
              time.

JULIE HOCHFELD, POET-TEACHER
HUMBOLDT COUNTY

Vacant Eyes Reflect

when I saw her
sitting on the bench
at dusk
in front of the library

i thought she was fine
just back from shopping, waiting for a ride
home
then I saw her face

not pink from sunburn
from lying on a beach in
paradise
face pink not from fuzz of a peach
flesh of a ripe
watermelon or apple peels

face of storms in some terrible wind,
hail, the blasted sun
a tortured place

she limps into night
flees the night like a bird

her hair dry like sand
eyes as vacant as a black diamond
neck furrowed like old bark

PAMELA SINGER, POET TEACHER
SONOMA COUNTY

A Yoga Summer

Linger in the pose
As aspens' anthem sounds
Could this life be mine?

Perseus showers the gift
of light in a zinc sky
Sparks my quest for truth.

Milky is the pond
Heart is a broken river
Chasing down the sea

Open to the sky
The wound is where light seeps in
Healing just hours away

Broken rivers heal
Flow on to bountiful sea
Giving, holding me.

Recapture the sky
Dwell on the sacred rocks,
Feast on hope, not fear.

Linden Berry, Poet-Teacher

Marin County

I Have Thought of You, Young Poets

I have thought of your faces
eyes bright with images
hands waving ideas on your fingertips.

I have thought of your frowns of concentration
your smiles of discovery
your journeys pressed onto paper.

I have thought of all the stories
wrapped inside you
each one a star in an endless galaxy.

I have wanted you to shine like that.

I know that you always will.

LOIS KLEIN, POET-TEACHER
SANTA BARBARA COUNTY

Our Mission

California Poets in the Schools empowers students of all ages throughout California to express their creativity, imagination and intellectual curiosity through writing, performing and publishing their own poetry. We train and coordinate a multi-cultural network of published poets who bring their passion and craft to public and private schools, juvenile halls, hospitals, libraries and other community settings.

Who We Are

As a pioneer in the field of literary arts education, and now one of the nation's largest literary artist-in-residence organizations, CalPoets recognizes the value of quality arts education for all students. Research shows that kids with high access to the arts in school are five times more likely to graduate high school than their peers without access to the arts.* In addition, in a time of fierce polarization, students build empathy across barriers when listening to each others' heartful writing.

Since its inception, California Poets in the Schools has empowered students to tell the truth and speak their minds through poetry. In poetry class, students experience artistic breakthroughs, accelerating personal development and emotional growth. Youth learn to listen beyond stereotypes while exploring the power of the creative process. A sense of belonging emerges in a classroom when kids are offered a safe space to speak what is on their minds and in their hearts. In this way, CalPoets' program counters divisiveness in schools and communities. In these extraordinary times, our work is more important than ever.

We reach more than 22,500 K-12 students each year in public, private and alternative schools, after-school programs, juvenile detention, hospitals and other community settings. In addition, CalPoets holds an annual conference, publishes an anthology of the year's best student poetry, and sponsors local readings and performances.

CalPoets, established in 1964 as part of San Francisco State University's Pegasus Program, is a 501(c)(3) non-profit organization supported by the California Arts Council, as well as by foundations, corporations, and generous individuals.

* "The Arts and Dropout Prevention: The Power of Art to Engage" by K. Brown
http://dropoutprevention.org/wp-content/uploads/2017/10/arts-and-dropout-prevention-2017-10.pdf